21ST CENTURY COMMUNICATION FOR INSURANCE AGENTS

BY ROBERT EDGIN

ISBN: 0-9911536-2-6
ISBN-13: 978-0-9911536-2-6

Printed in the United States of America

TABLE OF CONTENTS

HOW TO GET THE MOST OUT OF THIS BOOK

While it is possible to skip around from chapter to chapter within this guide to 21st Century Communication, I would recommend that you read it from front to back AT LEAST until you get to the sections that cover the different tools. Once you dive into the tools, there may be some tools that excite you more than others and it is perfectly acceptable to skip around between the various ones that will make up your 21st Century Communication plan.

However, the first three sections of this guide should be read BEFORE you dive into the different tools. I know that may be a tall order when all you want to do is get started implementing new things in your agency in order to increase your retention, get more referrals and grow your agency. The first three sections are like an instruction manual or safety warnings. If you skip the first three sections, then you will miss out on a lot of the underlying rules and principles that make the 21st Century Communication tools and communication plan so successful.

It's important to take a few minutes to in order to avoid most of the mistakes and pitfalls that you may otherwise encounter. Learn about the problems and headaches from someone who's already been there and done that - me! I've tried, failed and succeeded with all of the tools that you will learn throughout this guide. The first three sections will help you get ready to use them in the correct way, the very first time, so that you save yourself the time and money that I've already lost.

I've put plenty of samples and examples of actual marketing and advertising that has been used successfully with clients and you're free to use any and all ideas you see as if they were your own. However, it's important to have some fun and come up with your own ideas along the way too. It's important to make each and every tool you decide to use as your own, not just something of mine, that you're trying in your agency. It's important to embrace 21st Century Communication as a permanent way of doing business in your agency and not just a fad that you are experimenting with.

The tools you will learn about in this guide are not all-encompassing. It is also not a list of every tool you can and should use. Tools change with technology and trends, but the underlying principles and strategies of 21st Century Communication stay the same. The first three sections of this guide will help you understand those principles and strategies so that you can adapt to new tools and technologies as they are developed in the future.

If you come across new tools and new methods of 21st Century Communication, I'd love to hear about them and learn about the success you're having. Learning is a lifetime process and the more you commit to constant and continuous improvement in your life and your business, the more successful you will be. I can't wait to hear about all of the exciting and innovative ideas you come up with to touch your clients and prospects.

Finally, try to keep in mind that this isn't a sprint, it's a triathlon. You don't have to run full speed. If you start to feel that one particular tool is overwhelming you, it's okay to slow down. Everyone will pick things up at their own pace and you may be better at some tools than others. That's okay, just keep moving forward and you will notice big improvements in your agency. It reminds me of one of my own favorite sayings:

Run when you can, jog when you can't, walk if you have to and crawl if you must. Just keep moving forward!

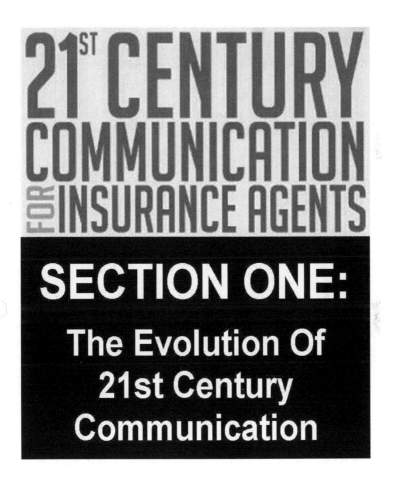

SECTION ONE:

The Evolution Of
21st Century
Communication

THE OLD ME - A LESSON ON HOW TO FAIL AS AN AGENT AND HUSBAND

I always knew I wanted to be an insurance agent. Weird, I know, but true. In the first grade when asked to draw a picture of what I wanted to be when I grew up, I drew a picture of myself holding a briefcase, selling insurance. In my sixth grade school photo I wore an Allstate Insurance shirt. I spent my middle and high school summers working in my father's insurance agency and when I turned 19, I started my own agency.

I was committed to being the best insurance agent I could be and I was successful from the start. I was the Allstate "Rookie of the Year" for my region. During the first few award trips I spent my time trying to convince the other agents that I was there on my own, not with my parents and talk them into getting me a beer at the company party. I was making more money than I had ever made and certainly more than any of my friends - most of which were still off at college figuring out what they were going to be when they grew up. By the time I turned 20, I had bought my first house, moved in with my fiancée and was expecting my first child. I was driving a new car and taking great vacations - I even bought my first Harley. But I had problems in my agency; problems that I never told anyone about - not my fiancée or my dad (who was still an active agent in the business) and certainly not my manager.

My first problem was that I was NOT a very good salesman. That old expression, "he can sell ice to Eskimos" was never directed towards me. I didn't like the pressure of having to close the sale and I wasn't comfortable with the tactics needed to hard close someone who wasn't ready to buy. I was good at talking to people and explaining things to them - educating them - but when it was time to ask for the order I would freeze up. The truth is that even though I sold a lot of insurance, I also lost more sales than anyone else. I was always amazed (and still am) at another agent's ability to overcome objections and fight through the "no's" until they got a "yes". I was only good at selling to folks who were **already** ready to buy.

Part of the problem was that I was too focused on the price of the policies that I was trying to sell. I made everything about price and as the saying goes, "live by price, die by price." I thought that in order to sell a policy, I had to be cheaper than their current company and the only thing I focused on was saving people money. As I'm sure you're aware, this mindset does NOT bring in the best type of clientele. If I quoted someone's insurance package and was higher than their current insurance, half the time I just gave up and didn't even bother calling the prospect back to give them the quote. The only reason I was successful was because I talked to more people and quoted more insurance than any other agents. I put 10 business cards in my pocket every morning and didn't go home until I gave them all out. I went to car dealerships, apartment complexes, townhome communities and new home sites and passed out card after card after card in order to find enough people who would let me give them a proposal and, fortunately, my price was lower often enough that I sold a decent amount of insurance.

I never knew where my next sale was going to come from because I was too focused on the wrong thing! I woke up every morning thinking that my job was to go pound the pavement and chase sales. I was a door to door salesman. In months where I knocked on enough doors and came across enough people who were paying more for their insurance, I made a lot of sales. However, if I took a vacation, missed work or talked to too many people who were paying less, my sales suffered. In order to make sure I hit my numbers each month, I worked myself to death. Monday through Thursday, I stayed at the office until 7:30 p.m. making cold calls to homeowners asking them if I could mail them a proposal for their home insurance. Every Saturday morning, I was in my office making more calls or out visiting car dealerships and passing out more business cards.

The bottom line is that I was successful because I had no life. I worked longer than anyone else and harder than anyone else. That was my secret. I was a very opportunistic agent, completely focused on the next sale. I thought that if I could just work a little harder and stay focused on the next sale that eventually things would get easier, but they never did. In fact, staying focused on the next sale and talking to so many new people actually made things harder and contributed to the second big problem in my agency - customer service.

As my agency grew, more and more people started needing help with their policies. A change here, an addition there, people were calling my office all the time. The problem is that I was hardly ever there. If I was in the office, I was making calls or running quotes and I didn't want to take the time away from chasing sales to do something that didn't contribute to my next sale. I put things off as long as possible and neglected my customer service responsibilities. I was too dumb to know the damage it was causing in my agency and since I was still putting a lot of new clients on the books, management either didn't notice my shrinking retention rate or chose to look the other way.

I eventually broke down and hired a customer service rep to watch the office and help out while I was chasing the next sale but even that wasn't enough. I had to spend more and more time in the office fixing problems which left less time during the day to get out and knock on doors. My solution to the problem seemed pretty obvious, work harder! Instead of quitting at 7:30 at night, I extended my hours to 9:00. Instead of working Saturday mornings, I worked the entire day. On the rare occasions that I took time away for dinner or a movie with my lovely fiancée, I would carry my cell phone, laptop and interrupt whatever I was doing if someone called in looking to get an insurance quote. Although my personal life was getting tougher, my sales were picking back up.

I was able to maintain my new schedule and extra workload by smoking a pack of cigarettes a day, drinking a six pack of Mountain Dew (there were no energy drinks yet) and sacrificing my personal life. Things were getting stressful but I was making sales and, since that was my only focus, I was finding ways to deal with the stress. I didn't know that as tough as things were, the really hard times hadn't even started yet!

Due to a change in the direction my company wanted to go, almost overnight, I was no longer able to compete on price. On the rare occasion that I was cheaper than a competitor, underwriting would have a problem with my new client and reject the policy. On the even more rare occasion that I was cheaper AND underwriting approved, the home office would send out non-renewals for twice the amount of business than I was writing. Credit ratings became a factor and when you work with clientele that are solely focused on cheap prices, credit scores are not always the best. It seemed that every day brought tougher conditions and higher prices. My retention rate, which was never the best to begin with, started to take a nose dive. Every new client that I had won with a lower price was now running towards lower prices elsewhere and my income was dropping fast.

Like an idiot, my solution was to try and work harder. Talk to more people, make more calls and knock on more doors. I didn't try to change what I was doing; I tried to do MORE of what I was doing. I found out that if you're headed in the wrong direction, stepping on the gas will only get you farther away from where you really need to be. My one pack of cigarettes a day turned into two packs. My Mountain Dew consumption went through the roof and my home life started falling apart because I was still focused on the wrong things. Eventually, my insurance sales hit a brick wall and in order to pay my bills, I took a second job. I gave up making cold calls from 7:30 to 9:00 pm each night and instead starting selling vacuum cleaners from 7:30 to 10:00 p.m.

I was miserable and my fiancée, now wife, was miserable trying to deal with my constant absence from home or misery when I was home. We were going broke and I was mad at myself for not being able to provide for my family. I was stressed all the time and a real son of a bitch to be around. The mounting pressures eventually became too much to handle and I found myself facing bankruptcy and divorce. When my wife and I separated, I hit rock bottom. Living alone, eating Ramen for dinner and missing my family, I finally figured out I was doing things wrong and decided to make a change. I didn't want to give up on my agency but I wasn't going to throw away my personal life to try to make it a success. I knew that there was a better way to get ahead and while living alone over the next six months, I figured out how I was going to turn things around.

I'm happy to say that after six months, I made the biggest and most important sale of my life, convincing my wife to give me another chance. I made promises to her that I fully intended to keep, like spending time with my family, being there for all of the important things in our kids' lives and creating balance between my business and personal life. I made promises to myself too, like never taking my time for granted and missing out on an opportunity to tell my wife how special she is and my kids how proud I am of them. I quit smoking, dropped the constant soda intake and got healthy.

I also promised myself that I would run my business differently and start focusing on the things that really matter in my agency. I started working ON my business instead of just IN my business and realized that I could leverage the things that I was good at to build a bigger, better agency. Although I was never the best salesman in the world, I was a good communicator. I was a good educator. I was good at listening and making people feel cared about. I was also good at creating systems and I started putting plans together to communicate with my clients in new and meaningful ways. I started to use new tools to keep in touch with my clients and prospects. I became very strategic in my agency - focused on building relationships.

The hard work, efforts and focus on my communication have led to more success than I hoped for and the lessons I've learned along the way are the foundation of this book. I've found the pitfalls, discovered the shortcuts and stumbled and fallen along the way but I've discovered the easiest path to an agency that gives me freedom with my time and finances. I can now proudly say that I've been to every dance recital, soccer game, school play and activity that my kids have been involved with. I've taken more time away from the office to take my wife out of town or have some family fun than just about anyone I know. I've also grown my agency into a successful business that drives sales to my door and keeps me in the top 98% of all incomes in the insurance industry.

Now, it's time to help other agents do the same and help our industry grow at the same time. The tides have been turning in the world of insurance and things have been getting tougher for agents over the last 10 years. As tough as things have become, I believe that the hardest times are still ahead of us and the only agents that will survive will be the ones who know how to communicate in new and better ways. In order to compete in the coming years and grow your agency, you'll have to evolve from an insurance agent into an insurance expert, a trusted advisor. Using the tools of 21st Century Communication is the most effective way to become more than just an agent to your clients. It is the best way to become a valuable resource and irreplaceable asset to the families you work with and the best way to build a million dollar agency.

TIMES HAVE CHANGED, AGENTS HAVE NOT!

If you've been in the insurance business for very long, you know that it used to be a heck of a lot easier to be a successful agent than it is today. Have you ever stopped to wonder why things have changed so much for agents over the past decade? It used to be a lot easier because we used to be the only way that consumers could buy their insurance. Insurance used to be something that people didn't really understand. For the most part, consumers didn't hear much about insurance and if they did, they were being told to talk to their local agent to get help.

If someone wanted to get educated about insurance, they came knocking on your door or, more often, they just relied on you to put together the right kind of insurance to take care of their family. The agent was the expert and the agent was pretty much THE way to buy your insurance.

The only real competition we had was the agent across the street or around the corner. The economy was great, incomes were on the rise across the United States, more people were buying houses and cars and toys and there was plenty of business for everyone. If you had a sign up on the street and an ad in the yellow pages, you were going to make a pretty good living in the insurance business. Most insurance agents were really just glorified order takers, but that was all you needed to be.

If you wanted to grow your agency, it didn't take much effort. Increase the size of your yellow pages ad, buy a list of homeowner expirations from Statewide Data and start dialing, go visit the local car lots, home builders and apartment complexes - you basically just had to work a little harder than the other insurance agents. Since most insurance agents were not really working, working a little harder didn't require much. The same was true for keeping your clients happy. Back then, good customer service was the exception, not the norm. An annual review and a birthday card went a long way towards client retention and referrals. It was a big difference compared to today, where excellent customer service is considered the bottom level provided just to keep your doors open.

To top it all off, the insurance industry as a whole was in much better shape than it is today. Claim payouts were much lower and profits were much higher so rates were much more stable than they are today. People only saw slight rate increases every few years, not multiple rate increases in a single year like they do today. People didn't have to think about shopping for insurance all of the time because there was really no reason to shop. As long as you returned phone calls in a timely manner, acted nice and talked to clients once or twice a year, you were set! Those days are long gone.

The Industry Has Changed

Today, direct writers control the majority of all insurance policies. The last time I heard the statistics, direct companies accounted for approximately 65% of new insurance policies written each year. That leaves the agent force fighting each other for the remaining 35%. The top direct companies each spent upwards of 750 million dollars last year in advertising to solidify their position as THE go to insurance company for consumers. Flo is the number one recognized company representative of **any** company, in **any** industry in the United States. Geico's gecko isn't far behind. Agents don't have the financial resources to compete head to head against the deep pockets of the direct writers. Most agents do NO advertising at all and have NO presence of any kind in their local market area.

To make things worse, the majority of insurance advertising today is focused on commoditizing our products, services and the entire industry. The message to consumers is that every company, policy and coverage are the same, the only real difference is the price you pay. Local, professional agents are trivialized and shown as completely irrelevant, or worse. We are now portrayed as bumbling idiots and the hard way to go about buying insurance. We're shown on TV as ignorant monkeys who buy from the direct writers when no one is looking and then sling policies on the street corner to anyone we can get to buy from us.

It is the intent of the big, direct writers to put you and me out of business. Every agent they drive out of the industry is an extra little slice of the pie that they get to keep for themselves. There is a war going on for our very survival and we are losing. The truth is, you can't compete with the big boys if you try to play by their rules, but, you can outsmart them. You can let them have the ultra-price sensitive shoppers and go after the 35% of the market who want, need and value the professional insurance advisor. You can become a big fish in a little pond. You can show up differently than the big boys and make yourself relevant to your clients. You can become an expert, trusted advisor and provide your clients with the things they really want and need - which has nothing to do with saving 15% on their car insurance.

14

One of the great examples I see at staying relevant to their clients is Van Mueller. If you've heard Van speak, you know exactly what I'm talking about. Van owns a multi-line agency but spends 99% of his time teaching people how to protect their retirement accounts, take advantage of opportunities that the crazy stock market creates, beat inflation and lower their taxes, both now and in the future. He shows his clients how to leave a lasting legacy for future generations and how to keep their money in their family instead of giving it to hospitals, nursing homes or the government. Van takes "expert, trusted advisor" to a whole new level with his clients and, if you ask him, he never has to sell anything. I've seen Van speak many, many time and I believe it.

What makes Van so successful is his ability to provide timely, wanted information to his clients and give them the education and information they need to get ahead in their financial life. He brings his clients useful ideas that keep them on the edge of their seats and coming back for more. Van has an amazing 4 question appointment process that simplifies the work he does for his clients and generates more sales every week than most agents make all year. Van is a top notch communicator that always has people to talk to because of the value he brings to their lives. He doesn't have to compete head to head with any of the major corporations who are advertising nationwide spending hundreds of millions of dollars each year because, as Van says, "Now is the greatest time ever to be an insurance agent when you sell with knowledge and wisdom instead of data and information." To learn more about Van, go to www.VanMueller.com.

Consumers Have Changed

It's not just the insurance industry that has changed, consumers have changed too. Today, they buy on their terms, not yours. They shop more, compare more and educate themselves more on the internet. According to INC magazine, a whopping 86% of consumers start their shopping online in order to educate themselves about companies and products before making a buying decision. The truth is, most consumers only learn enough to be dangerous and still need REAL help from a REAL agent to put together the right insurance plan. Insurance is no longer the mystery that it once was and consumers feel like they are the king of the insurance castle.

Consumers expect a lot more than they used to as well. Everyone claims to have excellent customer service so clients and prospects no longer feel that great service is a differentiating factor in their buying decision. People have less time and more to do than ever before and are generally overwhelmed and stressed out. Consumers, more than ever, are looking for an agent that can make their lives better and easier. Even more than that, they're looking to be wowed and made to feel special.

There is also a lot less loyalty from today's consumers. They are constantly being told that there are better options available, that they are paying too much for their insurance and that you, the agent, are irrelevant, expensive and hard to work with. Unfortunately, most agents prove it to be true. Unless you're taking steps to proactively set yourself apart and be different than most agents, most clients probably don't remember who you are. They don't know your name and don't see anything different between you and the last agent they had. There is no connection with you and they don't see the value that you bring to the relationship. It's not that you are not valuable, because you are, it's just not being presented in ways that your clients can see. They don't feel the connection.

Fortunately, it is pretty simple to stand out, be different and make the connection that your clients and prospects want. We've become so digital, so faceless and so distant in our society that it is easy to build lifelong, loyal clients just by communicating on a regular basis in ways that they want to be touched and with information that adds value to their lives. The agents that figure out how to do it and make that connection will find themselves growing their agency while most others around them are losing business and going out of business. The strong agents will not only survive, but thrive over the coming decade and acquire more of the 35% of the clients who still want to work face to face with an agent. All you have to do to be successful is evolve.

AGENTS MUST EVOLVE OR BECOME EXTINCT

Times have changed, the industry has changed, consumers have changed, everything has changed…except for agents. I'm sure you know the definition of insanity; doing the same thing over and over again and expecting different results. Well, too many agents out there are going insane! Even worse than insanity is extinction, which is where most agents will be in 10 years from now unless they change and adapt to keep up with the changing times, the changing industry and the changing consumers. Think about it this way; if consumers are shopping for MP3 players, most agents are selling records. If consumers are shopping for tablets, agents are selling typewriters.

Is it any wonder that the average insurance agent makes $47,000 per year? Until you get with the program and become a 21st Century agent, you'll never make the income you really deserve and you'll never reach your full potential. At best, you'll be working a stressful job for mediocre pay. At worst, you'll be out of business. In the old days, all you had to do to be successful was work harder. Today, you have to work smarter and make better decisions about your business. Today, you have to treat your business like a business instead of treating it like a job. There are 7 major differences between the old school agent and the 21st Century agent; 7 things that separate the average agent from the truly successful agent. Although I don't have the room to discuss them all in this book, I do want to point them out so you know what they are and then focus on just one of the seven that is very important to the topic of 21st Century Communication. Let's look at them now and see where you fall in the characteristics of the old school agents vs. the new.

Old School Agent	21st Century Agent
1 Job	3 Jobs
Reactive	Proactive
Had The Keys	Has The Knowledge
Product/Price Focused	Relationship Focused
Salesman	Educator
Opportunistic	Strategic
Agent	Advisor

One Job vs. Three Jobs

Agents of old have one job, to sell insurance policies. Sure, they'll do some service work here and there (usually begrudgingly and poorly - after being asked to do something multiple times) and help file a claim, but that's just part of their work responsibilities. Their only real job is to sell insurance policies. These agents are really just salesman - employees of the insurance company(ies) they represent. They work 9-5 to make a living and, if they have a good month of sales, they make more money than last month. If they have a bad month, they eat Ramen! I think of this kind of agent as a worker, someone I could bring into my agency, provide leads to them and let them do what they do - sell policies.

If an old school agent is a worker, a 21st Century agent is an employer - a business owner. They are working not only to grow their income, but to **build equity in their business.** They still do the service work, the claims filing and the other busy work, but they treat their agency like a business, not a job. If you ask yourself, "What do I have to do to build equity in my business and create wealth?" your activities are far different than if you're working to make a sale and a paycheck. 21st Century agents realize that in order to build a business, there are three jobs that must be done. A 21st century agent spends their time on **client attraction, client retention and client ascension.**

Client Attraction may sound like the same thing as selling insurance policies, but it is actually much more than that. Client attraction is the marketing system that creates the opportunities to sell insurance policies. The first job of the 21st Century agent is that of CMO - Chief Marketing Officer - of their agency. As CMO, your job is to determine who your best prospect is - where they live, what they drive, how much they make, whether they are married or single, whether or not they have kids, what kind of work they do, what their hobbies are, what their priorities are, etc. – then, develop a plan to attract them to your agency, create favorable opportunities to meet with them and, ultimately, acquire them as a new client.

There are many ways to market yourself (a discussion for another time) that include building niches, running seminars, mass mailings, TV and radio, web sites, special reports, and on and on and on. You need to have a **Unique Selling Proposition**, something that makes you different than all the other guys out there and a **Unique Value proposition**, a way to relate your price as a value instead of an expense. You need to become a marketer of what you do. I relate this particular job to fishing. This is where you put the bait in the water in order to catch the fish. You need to have the right kind of bait for the kind of fish you're trying to catch, which means really knowing what kind of client you're going after. You also need to have as many fishing lines in the water as possible in order to catch more fish and a plan to get those fish into the net once they nibble on your bait (proper systems - yet another discussion for a different time). Once you get them in the boat and you've caught them, job two begins.

I think I've shown that **Client Retention** is every bit as important as client attraction but let me tell you a quick story about an agent I actually know that really drives the point home. Ken (name changed to protect the innocent) is a client attraction machine. In his region, he has developed a system for himself that brings in 3 times the amount of new clients each month than any of the other agents. He works very, very hard to do one thing, sell insurance policies. He's very good at it. He works evenings and weekends to run his system. He talks to more people each month than most other agents talk to in six months. He's a new business stud! He has about 1,500 clients in his agency and is currently maintaining an 84% retention rate.

Last year, Ken attracted 220 new clients to his agency. He won awards for his production. He was asked to give speeches about how he did it. He was seen by most in his region as an insurance hero, able to leap production requirements with a single bound. People were in awe of his production but...Ken's agency didn't grow last year. In fact, his overall client count went down from the year before. With an 84% retention rate, Ken lost 240 clients last year and, although he added 220 clients, his net result was minus 20 clients. Unfortunately, Ken believes the solution to growing his agency is to work harder this year than he did last year in order to attract even more new clients to his agency. He plans to spend more money on his marketing system in order to attract 260 clients instead of 220. True, this will give him a net growth of about 20 clients next year, but his net income will actually be less because of the extra money he has to spend to attract those extra clients. Not to mention, the extra time he plans on spending at the office and the extra effort and energy it will take him to produce the business.

Ken is increasing his output with no concern for what he's losing out the backside. He wants to grow his agency but all he's doing is working harder on fixing the wrong problem. He's got a leak in his tires and he's trying to fix it by driving faster! If Ken would take a little of the time, effort and energy that went into client attraction and fix his client retention problem, his growth would explode. Moving his retention rate up to 90% would net Ken more clients each year than the extra work and expense of attracting an extra 40 clients. He would see his income go up and might even get to spend more time with his family!

Growing your agency is EQUAL PARTS client attraction, client retention and client ascension. Concentrating on just one part may keep you busy, and it may even keep you in business, but it won't elevate your business or your income.

Client Ascension is the third job of the 21st Century agent. It is the process of ascending your clients from one line of insurance to two, two to three, three to four or more and finally to the level of all lines possible AND raving fan that consistently brings new clients to your agency. Client ascension takes time and a consistent level of communication that wows and inspires your clients. When your clients begin to thank you for communicating with them, you know you're on the right track. If something happens, you miss a month of communication and your clients call or stop by to check on you, you've got clients who are riding the ascension elevator all the way to the top.

It may sound too good to be true, but once your clients really get to know you as a 21st Century agent and start to believe that the new you is sticking around, they'll let you know how much they appreciate it. I used to send out pre-made newsletters to all of my clients. Here's a little feedback I received the first month I wrote my own client newsletter:

There are plenty of times every month that a client calls in to follow up on something I've discussed during the month in one of my communication pieces. They check in on my family and they ask for more details about a story that they've read online or in one of my mailings.

Once you get clients following you, engaging you, it's far easier to express a need for their family and have them follow through on your advice for a coverage that they are lacking. Even if clients already have a "financial guy" or "life insurance guy", what are the chances that they're calling him to check in on his family? Probably slim to none and that makes your job of bringing over all of their business much easier. I'm not exaggerating when I say that 70% or more of my annual business comes to me and asks me to buy. I'm not saying that I just sit around and wait for things to fall in my lap, I don't. I'm working hard, but I'm working on creating an environment that ascends my clients to the highest level possible, which is also the most profitable level for my agency.

Now is the time to evolve and elevate your agency. If you don't, you'll find yourself facing harder challenges and falling further behind. To be honest, it's the only way to save your business and help you to not only survive, but thrive, in the coming years.

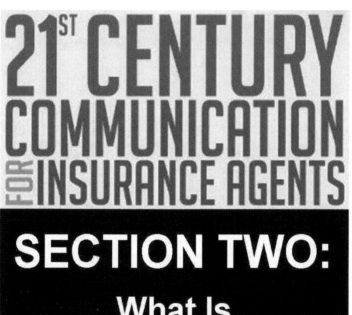

SECTION TWO:

What Is 21st Century Communication

WHAT IS 21ST CENTURY COMMUNICATION

21st Century Communication is the art of consistent communication with clients, prospects and target markets in new and meaningful ways to create top of mind awareness and position yourself as an expert and trusted advisor in order to grow your agency through increased retention, referrals and cross-sales.

What would life be like if you didn't have to chase new sales and worry about where your next sale was going to come from? What if your clients called you and asked you to sell them life insurance? What if your clients sent you "thank you" notes and called to check in on you if they hadn't heard from you in a while? What would your agency be like if you received referral calls every day and you had ½ of the clients canceling policies than you do now (even when rates were going up!)? What if ½ of the clients that did leave your agency came back? It's all possible when you run your agency with 21st Century Communication.

21st Century Communication is more than just the tools to use with your clients, it is a change in mindset and a shift of focus in your agency. It creates a new environment of trust, advice, education and options for your clients. It leads to better relationships and building relationships is the true business that we are in. It is, at least, if you don't want to be competing with the Geicos and Progressives of the world for customers who constantly shop for the cheapest price and will leave your agency to save $1 a month!

Let me put things in a different perspective for you. If you've been running your agency like most agents, you've been looking for clients to date. You get together with them once or twice, find out just enough insignificant things about them to have a little fun and either get a little lucky (if you can get them to buy something) or strike out (if they don't buy). 21st Century agents, on the other hand, create life-long relationships with their clients. Master marketer Dan Kennedy poses this question about client relationships: "What will this relationship have to look like for this customer to stay married to you for life?" What will you need to say and how will you need to act to create a lifetime of buying from each client you enter into a relationship with? Just like a real marriage, you'll need to prove that you're going to be there, you have to show that you're trustworthy and you need to interact in ways that keep you from becoming boring. Do it right and reap the rewards that a long-term relationship brings. Do it wrong and find your clients getting the seven year itch (or maybe even the one year itch), leaving you for someone else who makes them feel special.

It's really not that tough to figure out the things that need to be done to sustain a long-term marriage with your clients but most agents are unwilling to take the time to do it. At the heart of all great marriages is great communication; authentic, engaging communication that keeps your spouse happy to see you and hear from you; communication that brings value to your relationship and enjoyment for both parties; communication that creates trust and a sense of loyalty. Great marriages also need a foundation of trust in order to last. Just like a spouse, your clients need to trust that you know what you're talking about and have their best interests at heart. They need to trust in your advice and opinions or they'll never take your advice and buy the products you know they need to protect their family. They need to trust that you are worth the money they give your agency and your company every month.

21st Century Communication lays the groundwork for a healthy, long-term relationship with your clients by answering seven questions that every client wants to know about working with you:

1. Is this agent **Authentic?**
2. Is this agent **Believable?**
3. Is this agent **Knowledgeable and Competent?**
4. Is this agent **Listening To What I Really Need?**
5. Is this agent **The Best Choice vs. Other AGENTS?**
6. Is this agent **Properly Protecting Me?**
7. Is this agent offering me a **Fair Price?**

Out of the 7 things that your clients and prospects want to know about working with you, only one pertains to product and only one pertains to price. The other 5 are about you and the relationship they expect to have with their agent. A price increase may prompt a prospect to start shopping for insurance, leading them to you for a proposal, but price is only ONE of the deciding factors in choosing you as their agent. Prospects and clients will talk about price because people have been trained to talk about price when they are buying something. However, if that is what YOU focus on, you're missing the boat on the other 6 questions that need to be answered.

What clients and prospects really want is help! There are FAR too many choices and decisions that have to be made in someone's insurance program for them to competently evaluate them all. Consumers are overworked, short on time and up to their eyeballs in decisions that have to be made every day. Most of them don't want to take the time to educate themselves on the proper coverage, the right and wrong insurance policies or even evaluate who is going to have the best value for their family. It is far easier to choose a person they can trust and rely on - an expert - and leave the decisions up to them. That's where you come in and why 21st Century Communication is so vital. It delivers EXACTLY what clients and prospects are really looking for. Do a good job of providing it and you'll find yourself with customers who are married to you for life.

Is this agent AUTHENTIC?

People admire authenticity. They want to know that what they see is what they get, especially when dealing with someone trying to sell them something. Salesmen have a bad reputation of putting on an act to make a sale and people don't want to be sold. Too many salespeople earn distrust from their prospects and clients because they are trying to be something they are not and it is sensed by prospects and clients. They may never be able to put their finger on the problem but they can tell that something "just isn't right" and choose to work with someone else. Everyone has at least one trait or quality that can, and should, be magnified and highlighted for your clients (more on this in chapter 7 about perception) that will lend itself to easier selling and a feeling of authenticity.

Whether you're funny, intelligent and focused, cool, calm and collected or just a really nice guy, your best bet is to be your true self with your clients. This does not mean that you show up for work in shorts and sandals, having just crawled out of bed from a night out on the town. You do have to dress for success and make sure your office presentable. However, if you're really a jokester who likes to make people laugh, then you shouldn't spend your time with clients being straight-faced and serious, holding back every joke that comes to mind and trying to be the proper agent you think you should be. Yes, there is a balance that needs to be maintained (it's hard to sell insurance if you're putting on a 20 minute comedy routine) but your clients and prospects will sense that you are not being your true self and will have a gut feeling of mistrust towards you and that's bad for business!

Is this agent BELIEVABLE?

People want to know that you are telling them the truth. This is different than if you are being true to yourself. This is about being true to your clients and prospects. Obviously, good agents tell their clients the truth. They don't run around lying to them about price or product or what is and isn't covered. However, most people have dealt with bad agents before. If they have not dealt with bad agents, they have certainly dealt with bad salespeople who HAVE lied to them about price and product. They HAVE had people over promise and under deliver and now you have to deal with it. Most people are untrusting of salesman and to most, you are considered a salesman. There are ways to present yourself as something other than a salesman, which the tools of 21st Century Communication will help you do, but there are also mistakes made by most salesman that make it harder for them to be believed.

Making claims that are too good to be true, presenting your products as perfect or flawless, being pressured into commitments you did not initially make or making promises that are tough to keep are a few ways that you will undermine your believability. The old saying, "if it sounds too good to be true, it probably is" is something we all learn as kids and most people have experienced things that were too good to be true more times than they can count. As an example, let's say you're working with a client who has the goal of protecting some of their retirement accounts. They've been burned in the past, lost money in investments and they're tired of seeing their hard earned money slip away every time the markets go down. However, they don't want to give up their ability to earn some type of return on their investment, preferably a return that outpaces inflation. As insurance agents, do we sell something that fits the bill perfectly? How about an indexed annuity?

A good indexed annuity will allow your client to participate in market gains and avoid market losses. It will grow tax-deferred and accomplish better than inflation returns. If it is presented as the perfect solution, no flaws and no problems, the client feels like there's got to be some catch that you're not telling them. Every product has a downside, every investment has flaws and pointing out both the good and bad of everything you recommend makes you more believable to your prospects. Approaching each selling situation as a chance to educate, inform and advise will let your clients know that you are trustworthy and not just trying to make a quick sale.

Is this agent KNOWLEDGEABLE and COMPETENT?

Obviously, you have to know something about insurance to get your insurance license. We both know that you know a LOT more about insurance than any client you're going to work with but it cannot be assumed that your clients and prospects know that you are an expert. Just because you open a roofing company and buy some fancy business cards doesn't mean you can shingle a roof. Just because you own an insurance agency and present yourself well doesn't mean you're knowledgeable about insurance. People need to see proof that you know what you're doing in order to fully commit to you.

Consistent communication that showcases your insurance or investment expertise goes a long, long way towards proving your knowledgeable with your existing clients. Ongoing messages that highlight your industry intelligence will help bring in future sales from your clients even if they are not in the market to buy anything when they receive your message. Think about this; you may not be in the market to sell your home, but if every month of the year you receive an article written by the same realtor discussing the most effective way to sell a home in your town, a video regarding the state of the real estate market in your neighborhood or a CD of a radio interview the real estate agent participated in about tips to getting the highest price for your home, you're going to consider that realtor to be an expert at selling homes in your area. The truth is, he may be brand new in business, but he presents himself as an expert, shows that he is both knowledgeable and competent and probably receives a call from you when you are ready to sell your home.

People want to work with agents that are knowledgeable and competent and they're relying on you to show them that you are. The 21st Century Communication tools you'll use highlight your expertise and let clients know that you're a true insurance professional. The right kind of communication makes it easy to show just how smart you really are.

Is this agent LISTENING TO WHAT I REALLY NEED?

Clients listen more and respond better when they know that you are truly listening to them and recommending customized solutions for their needs. Even though most people require very similar insurance contracts, everyone wants to believe that they are unique and special; that their situation is different than anyone else. In addition to good listening skills (a must for any successful agent), you can tailor your mass communication with your clients so that it looks very specific, as if it was sent to just one person for the benefit of that one person.

You can use shortcuts when communicating with both current and potential clients that allow you to shorten the amount of time it takes to provide personalized, customized solutions and answers to their questions, like video mail. You should segment your clients into similar ages and situations and create communication pieces that cater to the needs of each specific group. Is it more work to create multiple pieces for multiple groups? Absolutely! Will most agents neglect to do it because they don't want to commit the time and effort it takes? Absolutely! Will those agents who DO take the time to segment their clients and cater to each group be the most successful? Absolutely! Personalize and customize if you can!.

Is this agent THE BEST CHOICE vs. OTHER AGENTS?

There are about 400,000 licensed insurance agents in the United States (1). What makes you any better than the other 399,999? People want the best and are inclined to work with the best they can afford. It is important to present yourself as the superior choice in some category, for some reason. You need to be seen as an authority in your field because prospects and clients will choose to work with, and stay with, someone who has proven themselves to be one of the best.

You may not yet be the number one agent in your city or among the top in your company, but it is important to act as if you already are. I'm not talking about becoming some egotistical snob or power hungry agent that shows up to see clients in a car they can't afford, dressed in clothes they can't afford and treating people like they're just another step towards the agent's sales glory. I hate those kinds of agents and so does everyone else. I'm talking about being the agent that is known for helping more people solve problems than anyone else. I'm talking about being seen as an advisor that makes a real difference in their customer's life. I'm talking about being known for what you do and the niches you serve. Fortunately, you can CREATE this superiority in the eyes of your clients and prospects. There are 8 ways you can CREATE authority before it actually exists by using the tools of 21st Century Communication, which we will discuss in chapter 8:

- Authoring
- Affinity
- Credibility
- Familiarity
- Frequency
- Celebrity
- Referral
- Demonstration

Is this agent PROPERLY PROTECTING ME?

A new prospect may talk about the importance of lowest price as a defensive mechanism against being sold things they don't need but what most people really care about is the protection of their family and assets (especially if you're working with the right kind of clients). No one really likes to buy insurance but they like what insurance does for them if they ever need it. Clients want to know that the agent they have chosen is an agent who is focused on truly protecting them. People want **customized solutions** for their specific needs.

Too many agents focus on what insurance is and forget to talk about all of things it does. You should present an insurance proposal for all of the things it will do for the person you are talking to - their specific house, cars, assets, family and how each coverage will benefit their family and protect the things they've worked so hard to get. There are many tools you can use to communicate your commitment to protecting your clients. One of my favorite examples comes from someone outside of the insurance world.

Bill Whitley, a national sales trainer for companies like IBM, Apple and AT&T, developed a presentation for clients and prospects that he calls the "Your World Discovery Process." During a short but meaningful conversation with clients and prospects, Bill makes it very clear that he is there to protect the client's world and all of the people in it that the client holds dear. He creates a diagram of the client's world and points out all of the day-to-day risks that threaten the safety of his client's world. He helps clients realize the true job of their insurance advisor; to build a wall of protection around their client's world and keep out all of the risks that threaten it. Bill's presentation turns the average insurance agent into an expert, trusted advisor - a risk management specialist. Here is an example of what Bill's completed diagram looks like:

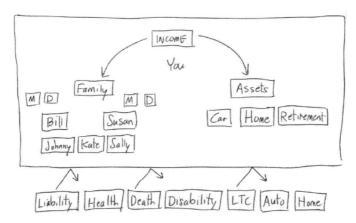

Bill's visual is a great representation of how a professional advisor protects their clients. To learn more about Bill or his "Your World"

presentation, you can visit his website at www.BillWhitley.com.

Is this agent offering me a FAIR PRICE?

Everyone wants to feel like they are getting the best deal possible; a good value for the money they are spending, but price is only the ultimate factor in a buying decision a small percentage of the time. If you are getting the best **value**, you don't mind paying the price. As an example, let's make plans to go out for dinner tonight. Let's figure out where we should eat. Option A is the best steakhouse in town, who happens to be featuring one of my favorite meals- a special surf and turf menu tonight. The head chef just returned from a culinary retreat with some of the world's greatest chefs and is itching to prepare some of the new recipes he discovered. It promises to be a meal that you'll remember for quite some time. It typically costs about $120 for dinner for two but because the chef wants to introduce some new recipes, the restaurant is offering a special package for two at just $79.99. Option B is the local all-you-can-eat buffet special. You just received a coupon in the mail offering you 15% of the already low price of $9.99. You can eat as much as you want and make an entire night of it. Where are we going to meet for dinner? If you're like most consumers, we're headed to the steakhouse! Even though the price is significantly higher, it still represents a better **value**! The food will be better, the atmosphere will be better, the experience will be better and you'll feel better about your decision later after the eating is done.

Agents make too big of a deal out of the price for their products and services. If your coverage and your office meet the needs of your prospects and clients better than their current low cost provider, then you are the better value even if your price is higher. Don't get me wrong, I'm not saying that price doesn't matter at all. That would be foolish. However, it is not the "end all, be all" in the buying decision. Consumers want to feel like they are getting their money's worth. Show them all of the things that choosing your office provides to support your price, whatever your price may be. If people feel like they are being provided with more than their current company and more than they expected, then price is just one of the factors in choosing you as their agent.

All of the things that people are looking for and all of the questions they ask can be answered in very powerful ways through 21st Century Communication. The best part is that if you do things right, you'll answer people's questions before they ever even ask them. You'll present yourself in ways that PROVES you are the expert, trusted advisor worth working with and you'll continue to give your clients good reasons to stay married to you for life. If you really want your agency to grow, this is one of the most important lessons you can ever learn - how to keep your clients married to you for life.

A MOST IMPORTANT LESSON ABOUT CLIENT RETENTION

Obviously, it is a good thing to keep your clients around for as long as possible, but why so much fuss - and an entire chapter - about keeping your clients married to you for life? Is it really that important? **YES!** It is far easier to grow your agency when you are not forced to constantly replace lost clients. The average retention rate in the insurance industry is 84% (2). If you have a book of business with 1,000 clients and an 84% retention rate, you have to replace 160 clients every year just to break even! Think of the time, effort, money and energy it takes to find 160 new clients each year. More importantly, think of the lost income from those 160 clients. Most agents are so focused on finding their next sale - their next client - that they overlook just how much a lost client costs them.

Do you know how much a client is worth to you? Do you know your **Lifetime Client Value?** This is what each client is worth to you over the life of your relationship with them - the total money you will make off of each one of your clients. This number is VITAL for a successful agency to know because it will help you better understand what you can spend to get a new client and what you can spend to keep an existing client. A successful agent should always know their numbers (their closing percentage, retention rate, etc.) and your lifetime client value is one of those numbers. In fact, it is one of the most important numbers. For example, if your lifetime client value is $2,585 (my personal lifetime client value), you can make some very important decisions regarding your spending on acquiring and keeping clients.

Most agents try to figure out the LEAST amount of money they can spend to acquire and retain a client. They are looking for the cheap way to grow their agency. Successful agents figure out how they can spend the most money on acquiring and retaining clients in order to grow their agency faster while still getting a positive return on their investment. Successful agents know that one of the secrets to growth is outspending your competitors on marketing and communication so that they can reach more people, more often and make more sales. They also understand what most agents don't: as long as you are receiving a positive return on your money, spending isn't really spending, it's investing! Let's do a little math based on my personal lifetime client value.

I know that a client is worth $2,585 in total income to my agency or $281 per year x 9.2 years. As a business owner, I have a decision to make about the money I'm willing to spend in order to acquire and retain each one of my clients. If I approach it as most agents do, I want to spend as little as possible. In fact, most agents want to spend nothing at all. If I take the common approach and spend nothing to reach new clients or keep my existing clients, I may get some referrals during the year and perhaps bring on 36 new clients (3 per month). If I spend nothing on keeping them, I can expect my retention to be the industry average of 84%, which means I can expect my lifetime client value to drop to $2,360. I expect it would actually be quite less because agents who take this approach typically have much smaller cross-sale percentages but we'll give them the benefit of the doubt for this example. Based on the math, 36 clients x $2,360 is worth $84,960 in total lifetime client value.

My other option is to decide how much I can spend to acquire more clients and keep them for longer while still maintaining a positive return on my investment. In my agency, I'm willing to spend one year's value in acquiring a new client and ½ one year's value in keeping that client - a total of $421. I know, based on my personal numbers, that spending $281 towards acquiring a new client will help me acquire double or triple the amount of clients compared to spending nothing. For this example, we'll use the low number which means I can expect to acquire 64 new clients. Because I'm willing to spend money on keeping my clients ($140), I also have a much higher retention rate than the industry average, so my lifetime client value is $2,585. If I subtract out the money spent to acquire and retain each new client ($421) then my net lifetime value of each new client is $2,164 x 64 new clients for a total lifetime value of $138,496. Tell me, which option did a better job at helping me grow my agency?

The $138,496 is actually only half of the big picture. We started this chapter talking about retention so let's go back to it now. Every time you lose a client, not only do you lose the portion of their lifetime value that you have yet to collect, you are also forced to spend more money to replace the lost client. In my agency, if I lose a client ½ way through our relationship, I'm giving up $1,082 in income PLUS the $421 spent in acquiring and keeping the client PLUS $421 towards a replacement client, for a total of $1,924. If you take a look at the numbers in your agency, you'll quickly see what a big deal it is to make sure you retain your clients for as long as possible using 21st Century Communication

THE 6 NEW RULES OF COMMUNICATION

In order to use the tools of 21st Century Communication, you must first know the rules of 21st Century Communication. Just like everything else in life, this too has rules. Trying to put together your communication program without knowing the rules that govern success is like trying to build a bunk bed without using the instruction manual. You may stumble through and get something pieced together eventually (hey, why do we have these leftover screws?), but you probably won't want to sleep on it. There are six rules of 21st Century Communication that will make sure your communication efforts yield the best results - increased retention and growth in your agency. These six rules provide the power to all of the tools you will be using. They are:

1. **Perception Becomes Reality**
2. **People Want The Unique and Unusual**
3. **People Need Touches**
4. **The Rule Of 50/50**
5. **Messages Must Be United**
6. **It's Okay To Fail**

You Create the Perception of You and Perception Becomes Reality

It's important to not only be **known** by your clients and prospects, but be known for something or as something. What is it about you that makes you different? Unique? Special? What is your **unique value proposition** that makes people want to do business with you? Here's some good news for you; it doesn't have to be anything extraordinary. You don't have to be someone you're not and you will easily create the perception that you want your clients and prospects to have about you.

Who do you want to be to your clients? The nice guy? The funny gal? The expert? Mr. No Nonsense? Mrs. Calm, Cool and Collected? For about ten years I was known as the "nicest guy in the insurance business." I was fairly inexperienced in the industry and was still learning all of the ins and outs of coverage and proper insurance planning. I knew I needed something to set me apart and help me stand out from the other 4,500 insurance agents in town, so I decided to BECOME the nicest guy in the insurance business. Just so we're clear, I **am** a very nice guy. I like people and I like helping people and, as I've mentioned, I've never been the pushy salesman that doesn't take "no" for an answer. Amplifying one of my natural traits and shining a spotlight on a part of me that people like (who doesn't like a nice guy) seemed like an obvious choice.

Becoming *the* nicest guy in the insurance business fit my personality very well. I changed all of my business cards and stationary to read:

Robert Edgin
A Real Nice Guy

I made pens and other knick knacks to hand out that declared my niceness. I gave my new clients gifts that stated I was "a real nice guy" and signed it underneath my name on every letter, "thank you" card and flyer I sent out. I created the perception with my clients and prospects that I was the nicest guy in the insurance business and perception soon became reality. I started getting calls from new referrals who told me they heard what a nice guy I was. Clients sent me "thank you" notes to let me know how much they appreciated working with someone as nice as me. I created a reality that allowed me to be different and standout from the thousands of other insurance agents I was competing against. You can do the same by choosing a part of you to become known for. The secret is in choosing a real part of who you are and then magnifying it; turning it up to a level 10.

It's okay to have an opinion that not everyone agrees with and it's even okay if not everyone likes you. A good friend of mine, a very successful multi-line agent and financial planner, is an extremely outspoken gun-loving, democrat-hating, far-right-leaning, hunting, animal-skinning, meat-eating outdoorsman who often shows up for meetings in his bright orange hunting jacket. He rubs some people the wrong way because if you're a democrat, he's going to do everything in his power to convince you there is something wrong with you. If you're a vegetarian, he'll try to get you to eat a steak. Needless to say, he's not doing much (if any) business with that group of people. **However**, he does a LOT of business with the people in his city who feel the same way that he does about your right (and duty) to bear arms, kill your own dinner and question everything the government does.

My friend understands that you do NOT have to cater to the masses in order to be highly successful. In fact, some would argue that you **cannot** become successful catering to the masses. He also understands that who you make yourself in the mind of your clients and prospects is far more influential than what you actually say to them. My friend has made himself an outspoken champion of everyone who thinks like he does. He has amplified his outdoor man, NRA status far louder than most people are comfortable doing and used it to become known for something.

It is important to know that you can also further your success by creating the perception with your clients and prospects that you are already the most successful agent in town. If you have a choice, who do you want to work with? If you or someone you love needs to have a heart surgery, which doctor do you choose? Do you pick someone out of the phone book? Off of the internet? No, you search out the most successful doctor in town. You ask your friends, family and co-workers if they've had experience with a good doctor. You choose the one with the nice office, large staff, degrees on the wall and articles published in medical journals. You choose the doctor with a 6 week waiting list because there are so many people lined up to see him.

Granted, our offerings are not quite as life and death as the heart surgeons, but people still want to work with successful people in every industry, including ours. You can create a perception of success that becomes reality. If you act like the most successful agent in town, it's just a matter of time before you *are* the most successful agent in town. I'm not talking about an out of control ego or driving around in a Porsche that you can't even afford to put gas in. I'm talking about dressing, talking and acting as if you are already accomplished and presenting yourself as a valuable resource that your prospects would be lucky to work with and not some needy salesman who is chasing the sale in order to be able to eat tonight. People want to know who they are working with and they want to work with a successful agent. Create the perception of who you want to be and it will become reality with your clients and prospects. Who you have made yourself in the mind of your prospects and clients is far more influential than anything you can say.

People Want the Unique/Unusual

I want to share two facts about people that will help clarify why people want the unusual. First, most people's everyday lives are pretty boring. They get up, get the kids ready for school, go to work, come home, eat dinner, watch TV, go to bed and then get up the next day and do it all over again. They're overworked and underpaid and don't get to live the exciting lives they once dreamed about. This is why you run into an old friend after 10 years apart and have them tell you there's nothing new in their life, "just work and kids, the same old stuff." Most people are looking for distractions and entertainment in order to escape the monotony of everyday life. Movies and restaurants continue to do well regardless of any recession we might be facing because people need an escape. This is a very important point that you can, and will, use in your favor.

Second, people are also callused. They're callused to advertising, salesman and hard closes. They've seen so many companies and people shouting from the rooftops that they are better, their product is better and that everyone else is more expensive, that they no longer listen to what they are being told in advertisements. A salesman is a salesman, regardless of what they are selling and most people have seen enough salesmen for two lifetimes before you ever come into their lives. People don't want to listen to what any salesman has to say and they certainly don't believe most of what they hear. This may sound bad, but for you this is actually a very good thing and something that you will also use in your favor.

People want to be wowed, entertained and made to feel special. They want to see things they have not seen before and are drawn to the unusual and different. Geico and Progressive understand this principle better than just about anyone and everyone in the insurance industry. That's why they spend hundreds of millions of dollars a year entertaining people with talking pigs and lizards. They're giving people something different, something they haven't seen before - especially when it comes to insurance. They're distracting people from their everyday lives for a few minutes and giving them a 30 second escape from reality.

You and I will never have the resources to approach people the way that the big boys do but you can still set yourself apart from the competition by giving your clients the unique and unusual. The first key is to make sure you show up differently than everyone else in everything you do. This is VITAL to your success as an insurance agent and a key part of 21st Century Communication. If your communication looks different, sounds different and feels different than everything else your clients and prospects have experienced so far, you're going to be immediately elevated in their eyes. It doesn't take a multi-million dollar campaign either, just a little bit of creativity and effort. For example, take a look at one of my communication pieces that is sent out to all new clients a few weeks after we secure their business. It's called the "Something Popped Up" campaign:

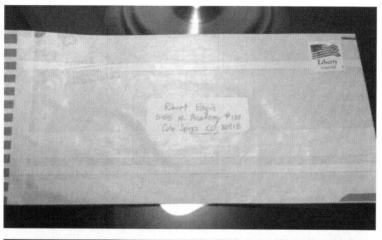

Our "Something Popped Up" campaign includes a popcorn bag, a mini bag of microwave popcorn and a letter that introduces another line of business that was not sold in our initial meeting. If we initially sold an auto and home policy, our popcorn mailer discusses an umbrella policy. If we already sold the umbrella, we talk about life insurance. We have multiple mailers ready to go and the only thing that has to be decided is which one is appropriate for each client. The communication to the client is simple and straightforward - as we were processing their new applications, the thought popped up that we completely forgot to mention...whatever line we did not sell. The overall cost for the bag, popcorn, printing and mailing is about $2.00 per client, a heck of a lot less than the hundreds of millions that the big boys spent on their TV commercials but every bit as unique and unusual.

The second key is to be fascinating to your clients. People are more apt to listen to what you have to say if you fascinate them and deliver your message in a unique or unusual way. There are many ways to be fascinating, and you can do it with any personality type. You don't have to be a celebrity, socialite or millionaire to fascinate people. Sally Hogshead has dedicated an entire book to finding your own ways to fascinate people called, appropriately enough, "Fascinate." (3) Here's what Sally has to say about being fascinating:

"In a distracted, overcrowded world, how do certain leaders, friends, and family members convince you to change your behavior? Fascination: the most powerful way to influence decision making… Fascination plays a role in every type of decision making, from the brands you choose to the songs you remember, from the person you marry to the employees you hire. And by activating the right triggers, you can make anything become fascinating"

Living out some type of adventure and then sharing the experience is one way to make a connection and keep your clients interested in you and what you have to say. You're probably agreeing with me that it makes sense to be fascinating but questioning your ability to fascinate. Fortunately, it is really much simpler than most agents imagine. I was recently having this same conversation with a good friend of mine and fellow multi-line agent, Martin (name changed). He was telling me that he does not have the opportunity to share things with his clients and communicate as often as I do because nothing ever happens in his life that is worth sharing. He told me that he was not fascinating and that I had it much easier because there was always something going on in my life worth sharing.

Martin fell into the same trap that most agents, prospects and clients fall into. They think their life is boring. I reminded Martin that over the past year he had been on numerous vacations (including a two week trip to Asia), he had purchased a rental property, taken on a new office partner, gone to several concerts, lost some money in Vegas, won some awards, found a new restaurant he loved, bought a new car, started shooting guns, celebrated his 5 year anniversary with his lovely wife and went to more happy hours than just about anyone I know. All of those things could be used as an unusual and fascinating way to communicate with his clients and get them involved with his agency and his life. You will see a few of the not so exciting moments that were turned into sharing opportunities with my clients in upcoming chapters but for now, I'll just share a couple of the situations that I've shared from my life so you can understand how easy it is to be fascinating:

I spent the night in a Mexican hospital
My son learned to snowboard
My daughter cost me $250
My wife and I tried one of the new restaurants in town
My family went tubing
I taught my daughter to drive
I took my son shooting
My family and I donated some time to the Red Cross
Annual camping trip
I participated in a taco eating contest

Nothing on the list (other than the night in a Mexican hospital) comes across as very fascinating. However, when told in the right way, you can make anything and everything you do into a unique or unusual reason to communicate with your clients. Besides, **anything** you do and share is going to be more exciting than what your client did last night and far more interesting than **anything** else that another insurance agent has shared with them in the past. You **are** a fascinating person with hobbies and experiences that are worth sharing.

Give your clients and prospects what they want; a lot more than just a good price on their insurance policies (they can get that anywhere). Create lasting relationships by getting your clients and prospects engaged with your agency. Show up differently in everything you do and find ways to fascinate, entertain and wow your clients. You'll be amazed at the number of people who call you to check in on your latest adventure or share their own stories with you. You'll love the increased retention that accompanies your fascination.

People Need Frequent Touches

Don't worry, this section is not about your love life. Studies show that clients who receive consistent, ongoing communication (touches) from their agents refer more, buy more and stay longer. That makes sense and is easy to understand. However, here is something you may not know; people need to be touched an average of once per month just to remember who you are! Think about that for a minute. You want your clients to refer people to you and tell their friends and family what a great job you do but chances are they don't even remember your name if you're not communicating with (touching) them once per month! It takes even more touches if you want them to do more than just remember who you are.

In order to keep your clients happy, cross sell them and turn them into referral machines, you need to **engage** them with touches 24 times per year. You read that right, 2 times per month! A recent study by Advisor Impact, called *The Economics of Loyalty*, found that in order for clients to refer their friends and family, they must be more than just happy with their agent, they must be **engaged**. According to the study, clients are not only more likely to refer (see chart below), they are also more receptive to cross selling opportunities and sharing more of their wallet with their agent when they are engaged with the agency. What's the best way to get your clients engaged? You guessed it, client touches - 24 per year!

Knowing that you need to touch your clients 24 times per year and knowing how to do it are two different things. We'll spend the rest of the book dedicated to the right ways of communicating with clients and prospects but it's just as important to know the wrong ways of touching your clients so you don't inadvertently sabotage your success. You could pick up the phone and call your clients twice per month and reach your 24 touches per year pretty easily but it probably won't be effective at getting your clients engaged with your agency. In fact, it will probably train your clients to stop answering the phone when they see your number show up on caller ID. The secret is to mix up your touches, both in the way they are delivered and the content within each touch. You need to have a combination of customer specific, educational, appreciative and entertaining touches each year. You need to mix up your messages between information your client wants, things they need, and things they never expected - pleasant surprises.

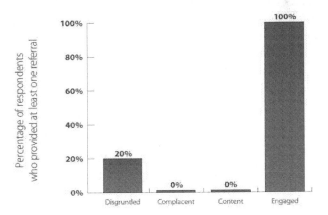

You also need to be consistent with your touches. If you start a monthly newsletter, make sure your clients and prospects get it every single month. If you miss a month or are sporadic in your delivery, it shows your clients that you are inconsistent and perhaps unreliable. If you choose to do a quarterly video or semi-annual review, get them into your calendar. Make sure you don't miss the events that your clients learn to expect and even look forward to. I was out of town for almost the entire month of February this year and did not put out a monthly newsletter. I received calls from dozens of clients wanting to know why they did not receive their newsletter and to make sure that nothing had happened to me. When your clients are used to receiving something from you at regular intervals, it's important not to let them down!

The Rule of 50/50

Insurance agents love to talk about insurance, just as all business people love to talk about their business. You spend most of your day dealing with liability limits, fact finders and life insurance. You share stories with colleagues about different coverage problems and underwriter issues. You work on case studies and talk about new ways of using life insurance for tax-free retirement planning. Your thinking revolves around insurance at least 8 hours a day, five days a week and you love what you do, which is good. Just keep in mind, not everyone is as excited about insurance as you are. In fact, outside of your circle of colleagues, NO ONE is excited about insurance at all!

Insurance is something people deal with because they have to, not because they want to, and most people think insurance is boring. Not only that, insurance agents themselves have a reputation of being boring. I'm sure you've heard the joke that if you want people to leave you alone, just tell them you're an insurance agent. If all you ever talk about and share with your clients and prospects is boring insurance information, all the communication in the world won't help you succeed. One of the biggest communication tools is "social" media. Notice that it is not called "insurance" media, "business" media, "information" media or "sales" media. You *must* have a good mix of both personal and business content that you share if you want to succeed with 21st Century Communication.

A good rule of thumb is 50/50 for your content split; 50% business, 50% pleasure. 50% for the things your clients and prospects need to know and 50% for the things they want to know. 50% work and 50% play. Your clients and prospects know that it is your job to educate them about products and coverage and it won't take long before they know that you are an expert in your field. They expect you to talk about insurance. You also need to give them the unexpected in order to keep them interested in what you have to say. The fun, entertaining, personal parts of your communication will keep your clients interested in what you have to say and keep them coming back for more.

Every month after I send out a newsletter, I receive calls and emails from clients about the content. During my annual reviews, I often get questions from clients that relate to my most recent newsletter. Here's the thing though, 75% of what my clients want to talk about has nothing to do with insurance! They follow up for the next chapter of a story I've shared. They check in on my family and other clients that I've mentioned and they share their own stories about similar topics. This is where real connections take place.

Keep Your Messages United

One of the best ways to make sure you are consistent with your touches and on track to reach your goal of 24 per year is by using a **communication**. A communication calendar will also help you with two of the most difficult and important parts of client communication - knowing what to communicate and keeping your communication united. I mentioned a colleague of mine earlier, Martin, who believed he didn't have enough interesting things to share with his clients. Martin isn't alone in his thinking. In fact, the most common problem that I hear from agents is that they just don't know *what* to communicate with their clients. They have no idea how to come up with 12 touches per year, let alone 24. This is where a communication calendar comes in to play.

Communication calendars have been used for decades by newspapers and magazines (called editorial calendars) to schedule and keep track of stories and articles from concept to development to publishing. They help keep printing schedules consistent so publications can make deadlines and plan out the best content for their readers. A communication calendar for your agency has the same goal. If you publish information to any platform (print, online, video, etc.), you can use your calendar to keep your content marketing organized and on schedule. A communication calendar is planned out in advance and forces you to think about what you are going to share well before it is time to do the sharing. It will help you organize your thoughts into a communication plan that now just has to be followed in order to be successful.

I'm giving you a link to access and download a sample from my own communication calendar, but before you jump to it, it's important to know a few helpful hints for developing your own - how to come up with your content, when to share it, how to share it, etc. First and foremost is your actual content and deciding what information you're going to share with your clients and prospects. To make life easier on yourself, I recommend planning your calendar 90 days in advance. 6 months is even better and having an entire year put together in advance is the best. I'm not saying it's easy, I'm saying it is the best way to plan your year. The further out you plan your calendar, the easier it will be to stay on track with what has to be done. You should at least commit to sitting down for an hour or two and coming up with your 90 day calendar. Then, at the end of each month, all you have to do is plan for an additional 30 days in order to keep your calendar full 90 days in advance. Here are the steps I use to put together the communication calendar for my agency:

1. **Start with the big picture - Choose a monthly topic**
2. **Break it down - choose 2-4 sub-topics (2-4 smaller parts of the big picture)**
3. **Find 4 points you want your clients to know about each sub-topic**
4. **Find one personal connection**
5. **Find one client story/example**
6. **Choose delivery methods**
7. **Choose irresistible offer**
8. **Choose call to action**
9. **Putting it all together**

Start with the big picture - your monthly topic: Not only will focusing on one topic per month make your life easier, it will also help you sell more by having an entire month dedicated to one united message. An entire month dedicated to a single theme gives your clients time to digest the topic you are sharing with them. Most agents skip around from topic to topic, sharing whatever happens to come to mind. But that keeps your clients skipping around too, never having time to focus on the important things you are bringing to their attention.

If a client is told one time that they need to consider GAP coverage for cars with financing, it might hit their radar as something they need to look into *when they have some free time* (after all, clients are busy people living their own lives and dealing with 1,000 things every day). If they don't hear about GAP coverage again for 10 months, because that's the next time you think to mention it, the client has forgotten that they've ever heard about GAP coverage before and starts over again thinking they'll look into it when they have the time.

If, however, you dedicate an entire month to GAP coverage and they hear about it multiple times, in multiple ways, with a personal connection from you and a client's story about how GAP coverage saved the day - they are far more likely to take action during that month because your consistent, persistent touches on the subject made them realize just how important it really is.

Choosing 12 monthly topics also makes your job of communicating and sharing a much simpler one. What's easier, sitting down for an hour - today - and coming up with 3 subjects to discuss or taking time multiple times every week to come up with something worth talking about and sharing? There's no trying to recall if you've already shared that information or worrying that you won't come up with anything to communicate. All you really need is 3 topics, one for each of the next 3 months. Once you complete the first month, you now only need to worry about one topic in order to keep your 21ˢᵗ Century Communication plan on track 90 days in advance.

Break it down into parts - your 2 biweekly subtopics: Every topic should be broken down into parts that can be shared over the course of the month. For starters, it will keep you from trying to cram too much information into one piece of communication. In these times of short attention spans and busy clients, you don't want to give them something that is going to take 15 minutes to read and digest. They simply won't do it. Instead, if you approach a topic the way that Reader's Digest does, with a condensed part of the whole that can be read in 3 minutes, you're much more likely to get and keep your client's attention. Think of each theme as a 2 part mini-series. You can even end a communication with a cliffhanger or a preview of next week in order to get your clients ready and excited about the next piece of the story!

Let's take our example of GAP coverage. Could you share everything there is to know about simple, boring GAP coverage in one piece of communication with your clients? Of course! Further, can you take it to the next level and break it down into multiple pieces, sharing and tying everything together over the course of a month? You bet! You can break down GAP coverage by talking about what it is, different places you can buy it, the difference between dealer coverage and insurance coverage, how depreciation affects the need for GAP coverage, how GAP coverage changed a client's life, how GAP coverage changed your own life, the top 10 cars that need GAP coverage, the top 10 mistakes people make about GAP coverage, etc. Even something as simple and boring as GAP coverage can be broken down into multiple parts of the whole and shared over the course of a month.

Find one personal connection: 21ˢᵗ Century Communication is about getting your clients and prospects involved with you and your agency. As the old saying goes, "all things being equal, people will do business with someone they know, like and trust. All things being unequal, people will still do business with someone they know, like and trust." (4). Adding in a personal connection to each monthly topic allows your clients and prospects to get personally connected with you and your agency. Seems redundant and obvious when you read it, but it is too often forgotten in the real world of client communication.

Your connection doesn't have to be a story about how you were personally affected or saved the day by whatever the topic of the month happens to be. You don't have to overcome and conquer month in and month out. In fact, I often choose stories and experiences that have nothing to do with the monthly topic but then find a creative way to tie them together. Back to our GAP example, you could share a picture and a little information about your annual summer camping trip. Talk about the hiking and fishing, the family songs you sang and the great food you ate (there's nothing better than cooking out in the woods!). Speaking of the food, your sister-in-law happened to buy the jumbo hot dogs but the regular size buns, leaving a GAP in coverage...which reminds me about GAP coverage for your car!

Find a relevant client story: People read and connect with stories better than any other form of communication. There are books dedicated to story selling because of how effective stories can be in relaying important information. People learn from other people's mistakes and they listen to others who have already "been there, done that." Try to find a client story that makes your client the hero of the story. If possible, show a decision they made related to your topic of the month and how it saved the day for their family. Interview them if they'll let you, use their entire name if they'll let you, and add pictures if they'll let you. If it is a private situation that they do not want to share, you can change the names and still tell the story.

Choose delivery methods: One of the biggest secrets of 21st Century Communication and communicating in ways that your clients and prospects want and enjoy is to use multiple forms of media every month and deliver content in unexpected ways. You want your communication to be a pleasant surprise, something that makes your clients and prospects say "Wow that was neat." We've already talked about the importance of showing up like no one else. Your method of delivering your communication gives you multiple opportunities to do just that every single month. What you say in your communication is very important, but how you deliver it helps grab attention and get people to listen to what your communication has to say. Your clients want more than just education, they want to be entertained. If you communicate your message in different ways you can educate and entertain your clients at the same time (we'll spend the rest of the book looking at specific ways to deliver information that really makes you stand out from the crowd).

In addition to helping you show up differently than everyone else, using multiple forms of media also acts as a multiplier for the reach and effectiveness of your monthly topic. As you break your monthly topic down into sub-sections and start delivering it in different ways, it will make you seem larger than life and give the impression that your message is everywhere. If a client sees you in a video, in print and online sharing different parts of your monthly topic it gives that topic a lot of power because it seems very important. If it wasn't an important topic they wouldn't be seeing the message in so many formats throughout the month.

A unified topic that shares different pieces of the message through a blog, a Facebook message, a LinkedIn article and a few tweets on Twitter - all referencing each other - creates a lot of buzz for your topic AND a lot of opportunities for you to touch your clients and prospects. Add in some direct mail, a newsletter and an audio CD and it really will seem like you are the only person in town who knows anything at all about…whatever the topic of the month is. Here's a diagram of what your communication delivery model should look like:

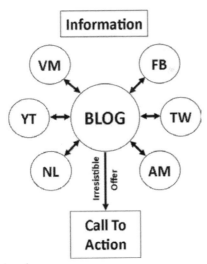

- FB = Facebook
- VM = Video Mail
- TW = Twitter
- AM = Agency Mailing
- NL = Newsletter
- BL = Blog
- YT = You Tube

You'll notice that in the middle of your communication plan is a blog. We'll be talking about the importance of your blog in chapter 11. From your blog, you can point to other sources and, most importantly, make an offer to your clients and prospects in order to get them engaged with you and your agency.

Choose an irresistible offer: The goal of 21st Century Communication is to grow your agency through increased cross-sales, referrals and retention. In order for that to happen, your clients and prospects have to be engaged in your agency and a great way to unite your messages and engage your clients is by getting them to raise their hand and request something from you. Every piece of communication you send out should have some type of irresistible offer attached to it. It needs to relate to your monthly topic and can be anything from a report or research study, book, video or audio CD, an educational experience, one on one meeting or a special gift - you're limited only by your imagination. You're irresistible offer does not have to be something that costs you money and can even be delivered through an email.

An irresistible offer is simply an opportunity for your clients and prospects to get something from you that they find valuable and will make their lives better. There are entire books out there on making an irresistible offer, but here are the 6 rules I try to live by when putting together my offer each month.

1. **Know your audience:** It's important to know who is going to be reading your monthly communication and tailoring your offer to match your reader. For example, offering a free report on maximizing your social security probably won't get you very many results if you are offering it to customers in their 30's.
2. **Make your offer very clear and simple**: People must be able to understand your offer instantly. Confused people do not respond and people are confused easily.
3. **Alleviate pain and satisfy desires:** The two biggest motivators for people are alleviating pain or satisfying a desire. People must understand what your offer is going to do for them and how it will make their life better. What specific problem can you help them solve (what pain can you take away)? What specific way can you help them get ahead in life? Give them one in your monthly offer.
4. **There must be a good reason you are making the offer:** If you give something away without explaining why, you create skepticism and suspicion. People have heard all their lives that there is no such thing as a free lunch. The explanation can be as simple as a way of

bringing more value to your client relationships, a way to introduce a new part of your practice to your clients or a way to say "thank you". Just about any explanation will do.

5. **The offer must be perceived as valuable:** Even for something that is free and relatively easy to get, no one is going to raise their hand for your monthly offer if it does not seem valuable. One way to add value is through social proof; "over 40,000 people across the country have used this method of evaluating and maximizing their social security." You can also show the dollar value of your irresistible offer, even if it's not being sold in stores or it is something you created (A $19.95 value!)

6. **Make it easy to respond:** The easier you make it for someone to raise their hand for your monthly offer, the more responses you will get. You should create as many ways as possible for your clients and prospects to respond. Allow them to call your office, call a dedicated number to leave their name and info, sign up on line, and mail back a postage-paid response card, email, fax or anything else you can think of.

Choose a call to action: You want to require the smallest amount of information needed in order to provide your irresistible offer to your clients and prospects. Start simple and don't require too much or you'll prevent people from raising their hand for your offer. HOWEVER, you MUST have an actual call to action. You MUST ask your clients and prospects to do something that is the equivalent of raising their hand. This is what separates your clients and prospects that are interested from those who are not so you know who to concentrate your efforts on and who you have a shot of selling something to. Don't let anyone get your monthly offer unless they specifically request it.

Every time someone raises their hand for your monthly irresistible offer, you know you have a potential sale waiting for you with that client or prospect. A monthly themed offer will provide you with leads every month and better yet, the leads are coming to you and asking you for information. Every year, a minimum of 50% of my business asks to buy from me. I don't have to chase them down, cold call or buy leads because I have a continuous stream of clients and prospects requesting my monthly themed irresistible offer. All you have to do is create the right environment in your agency to do the same.

Putting it all together: Your communication calendar is ready to be put into action, now all you have to do is plan out your work and then commit to working your plan. Until you can work up to a 90 day calendar, take it one month at a time and choose as many delivery methods and different ways of communicating as you can think of. You can see a sample calendar that I use in my agency by visiting www.BestAgentIdeas.com and clicking on the "**Book Owners**" tab.

It's Okay to Fail

Not everything you do will produce the kind of results you expect and hope for. In fact, some things you do will not produce any results at all; no one raising their hand, no one calling or even acknowledging your efforts. Even your communication efforts that completely fail are still a HUGE success for two very important reasons. First, every piece of communication is another reminder of all the things your agency is capable of. It's another reminder of the products you sell and the help you can provide your clients when they are ready. It prevents them from buying from someone else.

The second thing that failed communication does for you is that which we've been talking about since the beginning of this book. It sets you apart and elevates your agency to something higher than your competition. Even a failed communication piece counts as a touch and provides your clients what they need and require to have a happy, healthy, life-time relationship with your agency and be engaged enough to refer you to their friends and family and, whenever the need arises, open up their wallets to you for an additional need that you can help take care of.

You don't have to be successful in every piece of communication in order to have the most successful agency in town. All you have to do is remember the rules of 21st Century Communication and do what most other agents never do - communicate in meaningful ways that engages your clients. Now let's get down to some actual communicating!

21ST CENTURY COMMUNICATION FOR INSURANCE AGENTS

SECTION THREE:

21st Century Communication Tools

21ST CENTURY COMMUNICATION TOOLS

There are countless tools in the 21st Century Communication toolbox, just as there are countless ways to communicate with people. We are going to focus on the seven that are the easiest to use, work together the best and have the best reach for your clients and prospects. We're going to go where your customers are already hanging out and join them there. We're going to communicate online, through **Facebook, Twitter, YouTube** and a **blog**. We will touch your clients and prospects in their inbox through **video mail** and we'll reach them offline, through **newsletters** and **agency mailings**. In other words, you'll have plenty of tools to grow your agency and increase your retention.

You may be wondering if it is really necessary to use all seven tools. Seven new ways of reaching your clients may seem overwhelming. After all, there are only so many hours in the day! Don't fret, you're going to learn how to take care of all of your 21st Century Communication in less than 4 hours per week. Plus, you're going to take it slow - baby steps - learning and implementing one tool at a time until you're comfortable enough to move onto the next tool. You may discover that all seven are not a good fit with your agency or personality and that's okay too, but it is important to have multiple delivery methods for your communication. Seven ways of reaching your clients adds a level of sophistication to your agency that most clients and prospects will have never experienced before, solidifying you as THE go to agent in town. It will do something else for you too.

Everyone responds to communication differently. Some people like to read, others hate it. Some people are very visual while others are audial. Some like email, some hate it. The more options you give your clients and prospects to connect and engage with your agency, the more opportunities you'll have to reach them in the way they want to be reached. If you reach them in the way they prefer, your clients and prospects are far more likely to stick around, buy more and refer more. You use all seven tools because you probably don't know which of your clients and prospects likes which method of communicating. For example, my daughter is all about Twitter. She loves to tweet and be re-tweeted. That is her "go to" place for communicating. My wife might as well be named Mrs. Facebook. Yes, she has a Twitter account, but she loves to get her information one post at a time. Me, I'm a blogger. I like a little more in depth information from people that I consider to be highly knowledgeable. If someone has the information and skill to write out a 500 - 1000 word blog, that's the way I prefer to be reached. My dad, on the other hand, prefers a Reader's Digest type format - multiple stories put together in 3 - 5 minute sections that he can peruse. He's a newsletter kind of guy.

None of us are right or wrong in our preferred method of being reached, but if someone sent my daughter a newsletter, it would probably never be read. If someone tweeted my dad, he would have no idea of what to do at all. My wife might skim a blog and I may or may not see what you post on Facebook. By using all seven tools in the 21st Century Communication tool box, you'll have a better chance of reaching each one of us in the way we want to be reached and getting us engaged with you and what you have to say!

Online - Social Media

Social media is the convergence of technology and personal relationships. Never in history has there been such an easy opportunity for you to create connections and build loyalty with so many clients as there is now through social media. I'm sure you're already on at least one social media site for personal reasons, but if you're not yet there for business reasons, you should be! Simply put, your clients and prospects are there, you need to be there too.

There are unlimited opportunities to touch your clients and multiply your reach with social media, but it's important to realize that it is not the end all, be all of 21st Century Communication. Truth be told, I don't even count it as one of my required 24 yearly client touches. I count it as a bonus touch because there is no guarantee that any of my clients will even see what I communicate through social media. I may post at a time when they are not online or my tweet may go unnoticed but the opportunity to multiply your reach through social media is too powerful to ignore.

Just like all forms of media, social media needs to be approached with a strategy for success and monitored for your ROT - Return On Time - to make sure your efforts are worthwhile. You can communicate for no (or very low) financial cost through social media, so measuring your ROT is difficult, but you **are** investing your time. It's important to know what kind of return you are receiving for that investment. It's easy to get sucked into spending more time than needed (and more time than you should) checking news feeds and making posts, thinking that you're working but receiving an extremely low ROT. When it comes to social media, your time must be protected. The goal is to spend as little as necessary to receive the biggest return on your investment.

I limit my weekly social media time to two hours, one of which falls on the weekend. You can easily do everything that needs to be done in that timeframe, especially if you are using your editorial calendar to plan your strategy and scheduling your social media touches in advance. Every weekend, I use a free program called Hootsuite (www.hootsuite.com) to schedule my social media communication for the next week. Because I have a strategy of what I want to communicate, I already know what I want to post weeks in advance. Hootsuite connects to my various social media accounts and allows me to set up all of my weekly touches in advance. Then, during the week, I spend about an hour (10 minutes per day, 6 days per week) responding to posts, commenting on current events, sharing pictures, etc. It's a great way to maintain your relationships without neglecting other business building activities, sales calls and responsibilities that you have in the real world.

The rules for all types of social media are the same and you may choose to use some or all of them. Combining Twitter, Facebook, LinkedIn, YouTube, Ezine Articles and a blog can be overwhelming, but it doesn't have to be. Pick one or two that you are comfortable with and start there. As you get a better grasp of utilizing one tool, add in a second, and then a third. The more of the tools you use, the more **social influence** you'll create with those you connect with online.

FACEBOOK

The king of social media, Facebook, receives more than 750 million unique visitors every single month, with 63% of those visitors being over the age of 35. If there was only one social media site you could be on, this would be the one. It's the mega-city of the online world, yet it is extremely easy to communicate and connect with individuals and small groups. It's equally easy to measure your efforts and the effectiveness of your communication, making it a great place to start your ascent into social media.

You are most likely already on Facebook, but you may not have a business page set up yet. If not, this is the place to start. You may be thinking about using your personal account as your business and making connections that way. Don't! Your personal page and your business page need to be separate. You can share more things in more ways through a business page than you can through your personal account. Your business hours, directions to your office, mission statement, staff pictures and bios and a whole lot more fit nicely onto your business page. Plus, you have the ability to moderate comments on your business page and block people from your page if need be.

I'm not saying you cannot connect with some of your clients through your personal page, but it is a different kind of connection. People "like" your business page or they "friend" your personal page. Think about it this way; the people you "friend" on your personal page are the same people that you would invite over to your house for a BBQ. Would you invite some of your clients that you've gotten to know on a more personal level? Sure, but you wouldn't stand around and have a beer with all of your clients. Those that don't fall into the BBQ category need to go to your business page. The clients who would get the invite for the BBQ will hopefully connect with both, your personal and business pages.

To get started, simply log into Facebook and type "create page" in the search bar.

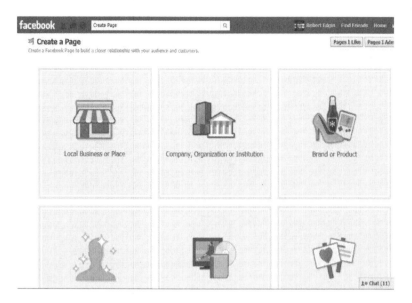

Facebook makes it easy to get your page up and running in a couple of minutes. Make sure you completely fill out your profile so your clients and prospects get all of the information that you want them to have. Choose good profile and cover pictures that you can keep as your "go to" photos and then change them regularly to help keep your page fresh and updated. Here is what my page looks like on a regular basis:

The picture above is one of my "go to" photos. It stays up on my page more often than any others. However, they are changed for special occasions, holidays, events and just for fun as well. You can tie your page in with the current events going on in your hometown or something nationally that you want your clients and prospects to know you support or participate in. You can see some more samples of my cover and profile photos on the next page.

You'll want to name your page once you reach 100 "likes" so you can give the page address to new clients and prospects. For example, my agency's business page is located at Facebook.com/MyInsuranceGuys. Most people simply name their name as their name (i.e. Facebook.com/RobertEdgin) or you can name it after your agency as well. You cannot give your page a specific Facebook web address until you reach 100 "likes". While it is important to get your first 100 "likes", it is equally important to manage your expectations about the number of "likes" you are going to receive.

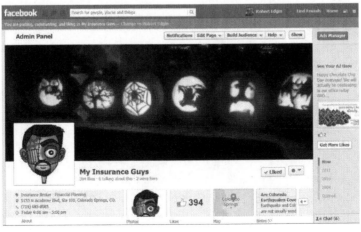

I remember when I started my business page thinking that it wouldn't take any time at all to reach my first 10,000 "likes". After all, if Ashton Kutcher can get 14 million and Lady Gaga can get 57 million, surely I can get 10,000! Unfortunately, that's just not the way it works.

At the end of the day, insurance is still insurance no matter how much fun you try to make it or how savvy you are with your social media campaigns. The thing to concentrate on when it comes to Facebook or any other social media tool is quality, not quantity. Are you getting your best customers to engage with you? Are you getting them to participate in your conversations and request more information? The clients who engage with you on Facebook will be some of your biggest fans, best supporters and best referral sources in your agency. The prospects you reach through Facebook will be far more likely to convert to clients and your retention within your Facebook group will be the best in your agency.

Not every client will join you on Facebook. Studies show that the average person will only follow about 40 businesses on Facebook (5). Remember, its *social* media, not business media! You're competing with fortune 500 companies and superstars that spend a lot of money and have entire teams dedicated to building a Facebook fan base. Thinking you can get even a fraction of the "likes" that they do just leads to unnecessary disappointment. I recently read an article titled "Insurance Social Media - 15 Savvy Agents and Brokers" that highlighted a few of the agents that are getting things right with their social media campaigns. The average number of likes for each agent was 488, a far cry from 10,000!

The first big question that needs to be answered with Facebook (and all social media) is how do you get people to connect with you and "like" your page? After all, it doesn't matter what you post if no one ever sees it. The first thing to do is to get the word out to your clients that you've gone social and then make it easy for them to find your page. Put a link in the signature of every email you send out that will take your clients directly to your Facebook page. Add the Facebook address to your business cards and as a P.S. on every letter you send. Have your staff remind everyone to get connected with you at the end of every phone call and make it a part of every client review you do. When we first got started with Facebook, we made labels with the Facebook logo and our Facebook name that we used to seal every envelope we sent out. You can even make special "social media" business cards that list all of the places you can be found online and drop it in with every policy that your agency mails out. You will also want to encourage all of your friends from your personal Facebook page to join you on your business page.

Once you've got the basics going, you can get a little more sophisticated with building your Facebook "likes". Contests are a great way to get new people to join your page. Everyone loves to get something for free, especially if they consider that something to be of high value. I recently ran a giveaway that rewarded one of my Facebook folks with a free tablet just for liking my page. The promotion ran for 4 weeks, which gave me plenty of time to get the word out to my clients and prospects. The tablet was valued at $239, so it was considered to be of high value to my clients and prospects, but I had actually won the tablet through a company contest, so my real cost was $0. When I started the promotion, I had 380 likes on my Facebook page.

During the first week of the promotion, I simply put the word out through Facebook about the contest and my "likes" grew to 394. During the second week, I included the information about the contest in a monthly newsletter and a monthly video email (both of which we'll discuss later), and grew my "likes" to 401. In week 3, I added the contest information to my blog and put some links out through Twitter and LinkedIn and finished the week with 406. I sent a postcard to a targeted list of my clients in week 4 reminding them of the contest, which added another 4. All in all, the contest cost me the price of one mailing to 400 clients - a total of $165 including postcards and shipping - but gained me an additional 30 "likes" on my Facebook page.

The day before starting my tablet campaign my page had 380 total likes.

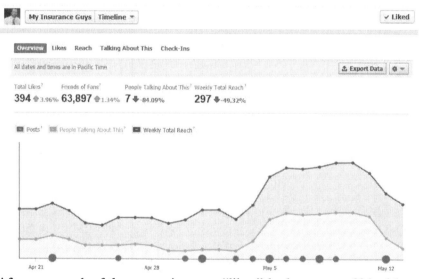

After one week of the campaign, my "likes" had grown to 394 with just a few mentions of the promotion on Facebook.

After the 2nd week of the campaign a newsletter mailing and video email telling clients of the contest were both sent out.

Number of "likes" after promoting the contest through blog, Twitter and LinkedIn during week 3.

Final number after week 4 and a postcard mailing to a targeted group of 200 clients.

Over the course of one month, I grew my Facebook "likes" by a total of 30 people, ultimately giving me the opportunity for better connections, better retention and better referrals.

One more recommendation to help grow your "likes" is make a big deal about it to all of your new clients. Include information about getting connected in your new client kit and follow up plan (not discussed in this book, but definitely a good idea!). New clients are the most receptive to your requests and recommendations immediately after joining your agency. This is also when they are the most at risk for buyer's remorse, so make sure you get your new clients connected as soon as possible.

Facebook Posts - How Often Should You Post?

Once you start to gain momentum and add new people to your Facebook page (or any other social media), you keep them on your page and involved with your agency by sharing the right kind of posts and information on a regular basis. One of the biggest mistakes that agents make with 21st Century Communication is a lack of consistency in their communication, including what they share through social media. While it is true that some agents screw up by sharing too much, the vast majority make the mistake of sharing far too little. You've done the hard work of getting someone to join your page, don't screw up now by neglecting them! If your page is not kept fresh and current, it won't be long before people forget all about you. Additionally, if someone is considering liking your page and the last post they see is from 2, 3 or even 4 weeks ago, there's not much of an incentive to join in.

Make sure you are sharing about 3 business posts per week and 3 personal posts per week, preferably one post per day Monday - Saturday. Remember the 50/50 rule; this is **social** media so 50% of what you share should be social. If everything you share is business, it won't be long before you have no one to share with. It is easiest if you schedule your posts in advance so you make sure you're sharing the right kind of things the right amount of times. I mentioned it earlier, but I find that the best way to do this is through a program like Hootsuite.

Hootsuite.com will allow you to manage all of your social media pages in one place. It will show you what you've got going on with Facebook and Twitter and allow you to schedule all of your interactions in advance! You can also see if anyone has mentioned you and set up searches for keywords that you may be interested in, like insurance. These types of programs are free to use and they free up a lot of time that you would otherwise have to spend going to YouTube, Twitter and Facebook making individual posts. You can see an example of my Hootsuite dashboard on the next page.

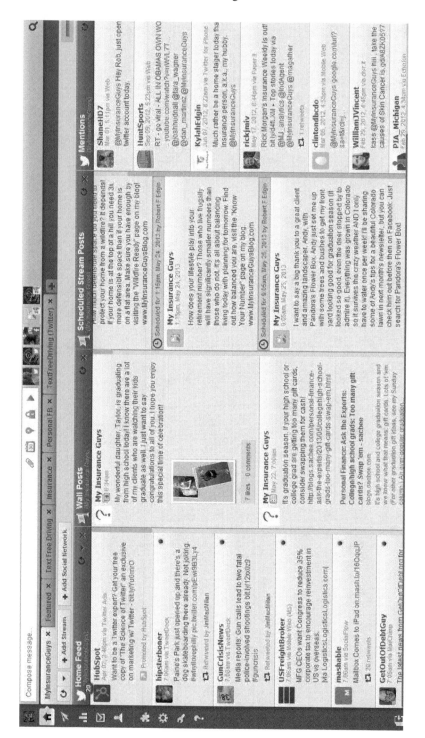

What Should You Post?

Now it's time to focus on the most common question I get regarding social media, what the heck should I post? I hear it all the time, statements like "I just don't know what to say" or "Everything I post seems so boring." Well, let's fix that problem once and for all with a few tips and tricks that will give you plenty to share. There are a lot of ways to approach your social media sharing. You want to provide good content in order to seem like a professional and build the perception that you want your clients and prospects to have of you but most agents tend to overthink and over analyze their sharing. You're not writing a book, you're sharing a few sentences (and sometimes not even that) to remind people that you're still around and keep you fresh in their minds. Here are some ideas to keep you sharing on a regular basis.

Be a part of the conversation that is already taking place in people's heads. It is far easier to join in on a conversation than try to start one. Besides, people are far more interested in what they're already talking about than anything you could come up with. A great place to start with your Facebook posts is the topic of the day - whatever subject that already has everyone's attention. The secret is to take their conversations and either add value to them or make a personal connection to them with your own life. For example, as I'm writing this chapter, it is graduation season. People everywhere are thinking about graduation. They have kids, grandkids, nieces, nephews or someone in their life that is graduating from high school or college. They have graduation on their mind. Here are a few examples of how I joined the conversation that was already taking place in their head.

65

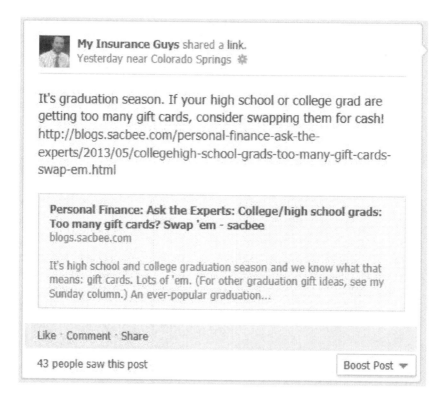

My Insurance Guys shared a link.
Yesterday near Colorado Springs ☀

It's graduation season. If your high school or college grad are getting too many gift cards, consider swapping them for cash! http://blogs.sacbee.com/personal-finance-ask-the-experts/2013/05/collegehigh-school-grads-too-many-gift-cards-swap-em.html

Personal Finance: Ask the Experts: College/high school grads: Too many gift cards? Swap 'em - sacbee
blogs.sacbee.com

It's high school and college graduation season and we know what that means: gift cards. Lots of 'em. (For other graduation gift ideas, see my Sunday column.) An ever-popular graduation...

Like · Comment · Share

43 people saw this post

Boost Post ▼

I made one personal connection, showing pictures of my daughter's first and last days of school and I added value by sharing a link directly relating to high school and college graduation. By the way, the personal connection performed 5 times better than the value added link. There are always things going on in your local area or nationally that people are already thinking about. Just because it doesn't relate to insurance doesn't mean you can't discuss it in your social media. School delays and closures, severe weather, beautiful weather, local events and national holidays, these are all things you can use to share something with your clients and prospects.

If you can take a local event and connect it to insurance, that's even better. Finding a connection between current events and insurance allows you to keep your page fresh, stay relevant with what people are already thinking about AND show off your professionalism by adding valuable information that your clients and prospects might not know about. If you stop and think about it, almost everything can be related to one form of insurance or financial services. Life changing events lead to conversations about life insurance and investing for the future. Severe weather ties into conversations about the claims process and what is and isn't covered under different lines of insurance. Here are a few examples of how you can make the connection between current events and insurance.

My Insurance Guys | Notes ▾

My Insurance Guys's Drafts

My Insurance Guys's Notes

Are Colorado Earthquakes Covered In My Home Insurance?

Monday, August 29, 2011

Earthquake and Colorado are not usually words you hear in the same sentence, but the recent 5.3 quake in southern Colorado is a reminder that earthquakes can - and do - happen. Fortunately this quake only caused minor damage, but if an earthquake hits close to your home, the biggest damage will probably be to your wallet!

Homeowners insurance polici...

View Full Note · Like · Comment

Serena Spell Great info Rob, thanks!
August 29, 2011 at 3:32pm · Like

My Insurance Guys shared a link.
February 10 ✹

In case you missed the story that Scott Harrison from News Channel 13 did on Thursday night about rising Colorado Home Insurance rates, here it is. I was fortunate to be able to visit with Scott and help explain why rates in Colorado have been on the rise over the past 6 months. http://www.krdo.com/news/Home-insurance-premiums-rising/-/417220/18459342/-/o1ibe/-/index.html

 **Home insurance premiums rising**
www.krdo.com

Many homeowners in Colorado have found that recent hailstorms, and not last summer's wildfires, are significantly increasing the cost of their home

Like · Comment · Share

22 people saw this post | Boost Post ▼

 My Insurance Guys shared a link.
December 20, 2012 ✹

Are your insurance policies ready for the end of the world? http://myinsuranceguys.blogspot.com/2012/12/insurance-and-end-of-world.html

 My Insurance Guys Blog: Insurance And The End Of The World
myinsuranceguys.blogspot.com

Like · Comment · Share

21 people saw this post | Boost Post ▼

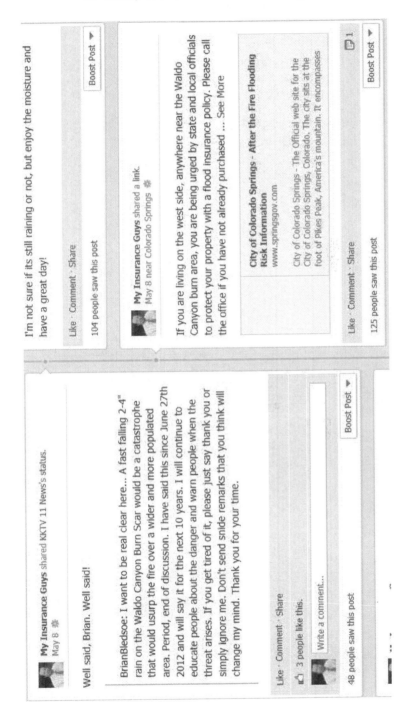

My Insurance Guys shared KKTV 11 News's status.
May 8 ☀

Well said, Brian. Well said!

BrianBledsoe: I want to be real clear here... A fast falling 2-4" rain on the Waldo Canyon Burn Scar would be a catastrophe that would usurp the fire over a wider and more populated area. Period, end of discussion. I have said this since June 27th 2012 and will say it for the next 10 years. I will continue to educate people about the danger and warn people when the threat arises. If you get tired of it, please just say thank you or simply ignore me. Don't send snide remarks that you think will change my mind. Thank you for your time.

Like · Comment · Share

👍 3 people like this.

Write a comment...

48 people saw this post   Boost Post ▶

I'm not sure if its still raining or not, but enjoy the moisture and have a great day!

Like · Comment · Share

104 people saw this post   Boost Post ▶

My Insurance Guys shared a link.
May 8 near Colorado Springs ☀

If you are living on the west side, anywhere near the Waldo Canyon burn area, you are being urged by state and local officials to protect your property with a flood insurance policy. Please call the office if you have not already purchased ... See More

City of Colorado Springs - After the Fire Flooding Risk Information
www.springsgov.com

City of Colorado Springs - The Official web site for the City of Colorado Springs, Colorado. The city sits at the foot of Pikes Peak, America's mountain. It encompasses

Like · Comment · Share   📄 1

125 people saw this post   Boost Post ▶

69

I didn't have to go looking for these stories. They were already taking place, maybe in my community or maybe on the other side of the world, but my clients and prospects were already thinking and talking about them. All I did was make a connection to insurance. However, sometimes you don't even have to have a connection to get your clients involved.

Every month there are dozens of odd and unusual holidays that no one ever hears about. Those holidays can be used for a lot of interaction with your clients and it gives you something fun and easy to share through your social networks!

My Insurance Guys ✳
March 14 via mobile

In case you didn't know it, today is National Potato Chip Day! Take a break from work, kick back and enjoy a chip or two - the number one snack in all of America. If you're out of chips, I happen to have 2 each of 3 of the nations top 5 bags of chips. Stop by the office and I'll give you a bag! There is Mama Zuma's Revenge, North Fork Sweet Potato and Dirty Mesquite BBQ!

👍 5 💬 4

Like · Comment · Share

Boost Post ▸

181 people saw this post

My Insurance Guys
Liked · April 16 ✳

Did you know National Jelly Bean Day is next week? In honor of one of the sweetest days of the year, I thought we'd play a little game of guess the number of Jelly Belly jelly beans! The winner gets the beans, and there's a $25 gift card tucked inside too! Vote here on line, email me your guess, or stop by the office if you want to see the beans in person. One guess per person please and all guesses must be made by April 30th. The winner will be chosen on the afternoon of the 30th and the beans must be picked up if you win. Good luck!

🏷 Tag Photo   📍 Add Location   ✏ Edit

Like · Comment · Share · Edit

👍 3 people like this.

📤 1 share

💬 View 8 more comments

Jason Burden 2412
April 17 at 11:56am · Like

Write a comment...

My Insurance Guys
Liked · January 21 ✿

I can't believe I missed it on Saturday, but happy National Popcorn Day (Jan. 19th)! I even bought some gourmet popcorn gift baskets to celebrate and I have a few leftover, so how about a little fun. Email or post a picture of you or someone in your family eating popcorn before the end of the week (1/25), and I'll enter you into a drawing for a gourmet popcorn gift basket, pictured here! You can email the picture to me at r.edgin@weinsurecolorado.com or post it here!

📷 **Tag Photo**   📍 **Add Location**   ✏ **Edit**

Like · Comment · Share · Edit

Write a comment...

There are other ways to be personal and have fun with your clients besides odd and unusual holidays. Start by filling your clients and prospects in with what is going on in your life and at the office. I'm not talking about just the big, life changing events; I'm talking about the day to day things that people may find amusing, entertaining or interesting. Remember, if you ask most people, they consider themselves to have a boring life. Seeing what you're doing might not seem like much to you, but it's exciting for your clients and prospects!

My Insurance Guys
Liked · May 17 ☼

We're starting to ride motorcycles in to work, which
means it must officially be summer!

🏷 Tag Photo   📍 Add Location   ✏ Edit

Like · Comment · Share · Edit

👍 9 people like this.

Write a comment...

My Insurance Guys
Liked · October 18, 2012

I've done my part and cast my vote. I'm feeling more patriotic than usual...I just wish the mail in ballot came with an I Voted sticker!

🏷 Tag Photo   📍 Add Location   ✏ Edit

Like · Comment · Share · Edit

👍 Ed Leyba likes this.

Jason Burden mine did, i thought it was pretty cool!
October 25, 2012 at 4:49pm · Like

Stacey Bayer Ziemba Lakey Yours did? Ours didn't. I want one!
October 25, 2012 at 5:24pm · Like

Deborah Levada I know me too mine didn't · Like
October 25, 2012 at 5:28pm · Like

Lee Rice Oh you have mail in ballots also. So do we in Oregon and I thought the same thought. Where is my Sticker
October 25, 2012 at 11:42pm · Like

Write a comment...

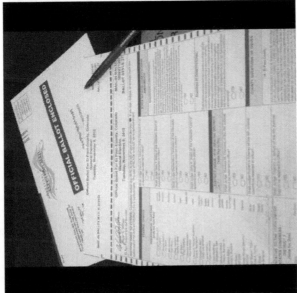

My Insurance Guys
Liked · October 25, 2012

The contest has begun!

🏷 Tag Photo   📍 Add Location   ✏ Edit

Like · Comment · Share · Edit

Write a comment...

Sponsored   Create Ad

$145 VEHICLE UNDERWRITER SALE

McCloskey Truck Town
Recipient of the prestigious CTADA "Quality

There are plenty of ways to have fun with your clients and prospects through social media. Holding contests and awarding prizes is a great way of getting people involved and your contests don't need to have anything to do with insurance. In fact, some of the best contests we've ever run have had absolutely nothing to do with insurance! Here are a few contest ideas for you.

We held a pumpkin contest - submit a photo of you and a pumpkin or a pumpkin you carved.

The summer vacation photo contest was a big success too.

Even those that don't participate in your contests will still follow along and pay attention to see who wins and your contests don't have to take a lot of work or require much for prizes either. The "guess the number of tacos I ate" contest winner received a $10 gift card to Taco Bell. The biggest prize I've ever given away (up until the tablet giveaway) was a $50 gift card. To encourage involvement in your contests, try to enter everyone who participates into a drawing instead of picking the best entry. You could also set it up so that everyone who enters the contest is an automatic winner, by sending out $5 gift cards just for entering. The goal is to get as many people involved and engaged as possible and contests are one of the best ways to do that.

Any time you can use photos with your Facebook posts, you're going to grab more people's attention. Facebook is very visual and gives you a fantastic opportunity to really make an impression on your clients and prospects through the use of pictures. People like and comment on photos so much, I started an entire photo album called "crazy about Robert or just a little crazy", where I upload crazy photos of things people have done for me.

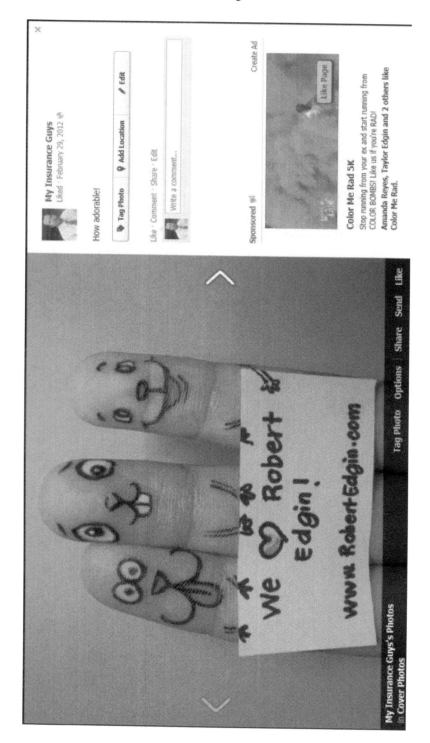

My Insurance Guys
Liked · March 23, 2011 ✻

Times Square - I wish I was there too!

Tag Photo   Add Location   Edit

Like · Comment · Share · Edit

Marvin Mullins likes this.

My Insurance Guys The newest addition. Crazy about Robert...or just a little crazy. You decide!
March 23, 2011 at 2:29pm · Like

Write a comment...

I always get a great response when I add a photo to the "crazy about Robert" album. People are always amazed that someone is willing to do the crazy things they're seeing in the photos. I'll share a little secret with you so you can get your own "crazy about you" album started. A lot of the crazy things that were done for me were bought and paid for online through a website called Fiverr.com. For a measly $5, people will do all sorts of crazy things for you! It's a great way to get some conversation pieces for your social media campaigns and some of the photos work great for mailings and other advertising too.

A great way to get your clients involved with you is to share things about them and their lives. Then, tag them in the post so they know what you are sharing. This works great for your clients and prospects that own businesses or have something to promote. It allows them to get some free advertising and it really solidifies your relationship too. Why would your clients ever leave an agent who promotes their business or gives them a little attention online? They wouldn't! In fact, clients that you highlight, promote and talk about often become some of your best referral sources as well.

Bob is a great client that owns multiple mattress stores in town. He was excited to see me posting about his business.

Steve doesn't own a business, but thanking him online for a great ATV trip he took my family on made him feel special and let him know how much he was appreciated.

Telling the world about Andy's landscaping business was the least I could do for a great client who took care of my yard.

Most people enjoy a little recognition and like to see their name up on your Facebook wall. Public recognition of an achievement or just a heartfelt "thank you" will go a long way with clients and prospects, so look for every opportunity you can find to highlight the people who do business with you. In addition to mailing thank you cards, I try to publicly thank everyone for the referrals they send to my office, as well as, welcome all of the new clients by name. Not only does it let the recipient of the thanks or welcome let them know that I'm thinking about them, it also reminds everyone else that we are a busy office that loves new clients and referrals! If possible, wait until you have multiple new clients to welcome and put them together in a post. Seeing a bunch of new client names at once makes it appear as if your office is doing a ton of business, even if that's not always the case. Remember, perception becomes reality!

One final way of coming up with things to share online is to simply share links of interesting stories or borrow what someone else is posting and make it your own. There are headlines everyday on MSN, AOL, Yahoo, etc. that you can link to or share on Facebook. If the word "insurance" is in the article headline, it should definitely be shared with your clients and prospects. You'll see in chapter 16 how to use these headlines in your social media blueprint to drive clients and prospects to your office, requesting more information from you about ways they can protect their family with your products!

There are a number of websites that you can access every week to come up with new ideas to share as well. Insurancesplash.com is just one of many websites that provides different comics, infographics, stories and statistics that are available for agents to use free of charge anytime you want to. Simply pick out the content that is relevant to what you've got taking place in your agency and paste it onto your Facebook page. If you have a specific topic you'd like to discuss, do a Google search and grab a few of the stories that are relevant and add links to them for your clients to access.

Measure What Matters

I'm not sure who first said it but the old expression "measure what matters and what matters always improves" certainly applies to your social media. Fortunately, Facebook makes it very easy for you to track your results and find out which posts do well and which do not. Click on the "insights" box at the top of your page and you're given access to all sorts of valuable information. You'll see which posts reach the most people and the demographics of the people who like your posts. You'll also see where the people live who are connected to your page and how viral specific posts get. You may be surprised to see which posts perform well and which don't (tip: posts with pictures always perform better!).

Final Facebook Tips and Tricks

Facebook is just one of the tools of 21st Century Communication, but it is a big one because of how much it allows you to do. Although you can't guarantee that your clients and prospects will see every post you make, you can make sure they'll pay attention to every post they see by following the guidelines that have been laid out throughout this chapter. Remember, Facebook is **social** media, so keep your business/non-business mixture at about 50%. Not everything you post has to be about insurance, nor should it be.

Share personal connections as often as possible and mention clients or their business whenever you can. If you do mention a client's business, post it on their business page as well so their clients can see the nice things you have to say. Share your thoughts about subjects that are in the local or national news. It's okay to have an opinion and it's okay if not everyone agrees with it. Avoid derogatory comments but be passionate about what you believe in. It will align you with those who are passionate about the same things you are.

Use your content calendar to plan out your sharing and you'll never run out of things to post, especially if you post them in advance through a program like Hootsuite. Adding in a few observations or personal remarks throughout the week is just the icing on the cake. If you want to post something spontaneously but are unsure of what to type when you see Facebook asking you "what's on your mind?" try thinking about it this way instead; "what has your attention right now?" Fill in whatever comes to mind.

One of the most important rules to remember about Facebook (and all social media) is that you must interact with your clients and prospects in order to keep them engaged with you online. If a client likes your photo, thank them. If someone comments on a post, respond to what they have to say. Don't neglect people and leave them waiting for a response or they just might not take the time speak up next time. Make sure you check your messages too. As clients learn that you are actually participating on Facebook, they'll begin to message you questions and requests. These are just like regular emails that clients send you so make sure they get answered.

Don't get discouraged if your number of "likes" isn't as high as you think they should be. Remember, it's about the quality of the connections, not the quantity. Your clients and prospects who engage with you online will refer more and stick around longer than any other clients, but not everyone will join you online no matter how hard you try. Just keep asking and keep looking for new and creative ways to invite people to join you. You'll learn in chapter 16 how to tie all of your tools together so that they feed off of each other and help you become a real social influence.

Facebook will do a lot for your business, if you're willing to do a little bit for yourself. Don't neglect your Facebook audience or your business page. Set aside one hour per week to get involved and you'll be amazed by the results, but if you don't keep your page fresh and updated, there won't be any results at all. Make the commitment to be involved on a regular basis or skip Facebook all together. There really is no middle ground.

THE TWITTERSPHERE

I have good news and I have bad news when it comes to Twitter. First, the good news; the rules for Twitter are just about the same as the rules for Facebook - only 50% business, complete your profile, use a lot of pictures, plan your work with your editorial calendar, etc. You can even link your Facebook account to your Twitter account so that everything you post on Facebook shows up in Twitter! Hootsuite, which we discussed earlier, will allow you to plan out and post to your Twitter account in advance too. Now for the bad news, although there is a lot about Twitter that is the same as Facebook, there are quite a few differences as well. The conversations are shorter (140 characters max), the tone is different (much more casual), and Twitter users value different things. Don't worry, with just a little bit of tweaking, you can use the work you do for Facebook to build up an equal audience on Twitter and really increase your social influence!

The first question to answer when it comes to Twitter is what the heck is it? Twitter is considered a "micro-blogging" site. Micro blogging is the posting of very short entries on a blog or social networking site. There are 200 million active users on Twitter, sending about 400 million tweets every day. Meaning, there is a pretty good chance that a number of your clients and prospects are using Twitter. My wife is really getting into Twitter and my daughter thinks it beats Facebook, hands down, because of how Twitter is used. Twitter is really designed for the "what are you doing right now" and "what's taking place right now" kind of conversations. It's more direct and to the point than Facebook and it's also much more laid back. Twitter is all about instant updates and the sharing of links and photos. It's a great way to drive traffic to your website or blog.

Getting Started With Twitter

Although Twitter is different than Facebook, it's just as important to your communication plan and, fortunately, it's even easier to use. Just like Facebook, the first thing to do is to set up an account and complete your profile, completely! Setting up an account is free and easy enough and I have no doubt that you can follow along with the instructions at Twitter.com. The only two things I want to mention regarding setting up your account is about choosing your Twitter name and filling out your profile. First, make sure your name matches up with your Facebook name so that the two accounts can be recognized as the same person or office. I go by My Insurance Guys on Facebook, so my Twitter name is @MyInsuranceGuys. That helps my clients and prospects know that it is me doing the talking.

Second, although I mentioned it already, I want to reiterate the importance of a completely filled out profile. Twitter gives you four things you can share about yourself; a picture, a header picture, your website and your bio. Your bio can only be 160 characters long, so take a few minutes and figure out how to say as much of the important things about you as possible in just a few characters. Try to make it match up with your bio or mission statement on all of your other media. You may be thinking I'm overreacting to the importance of completely filling out your profile, but according to a study done by Dan Zarella for his new book "The Science of Marketing", the correlation between completely filled out profiles and number of followers is undeniable.

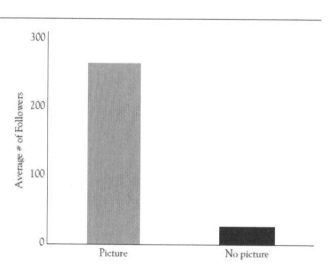

Figure 4.6   Effect of Profile Picture on Followers

After you get your account set up (it takes about 2 minutes, so go do it now!), it's time to fill out your profile. You can put in a lot of great info about yourself and your agency for your clients and prospects to see, so make sure you take advantage of the free advertising and completely fill out your profile. Add both a profile picture (of yourself) and a header picture (this is like the cover photo on Facebook, it can be a picture of your staff or of some type of message you'd like to share or something fun that you've been involved with). I'm not going to spend a lot of time here on the walkthrough of setting up your account, but I have compiled 3 of the best resources around for setting up Twitter for your business and I've made them available for you to download free of charge. Just go to www.BestAgentIdeas.com and click on the "book owners" tab. The password is **communication**. Here's what my Twitter page looks like:

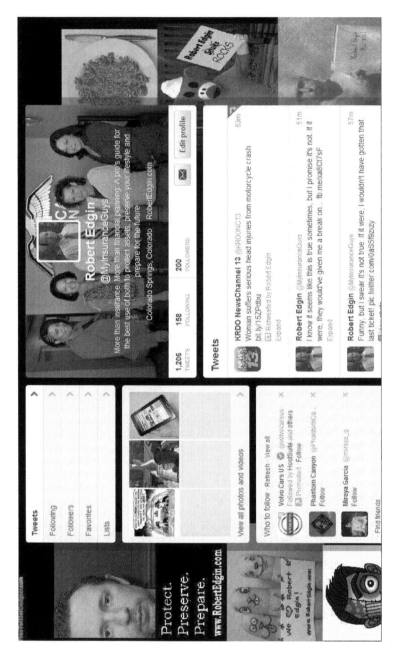

You can see that my Twitter profile and pictures are the same ones that are used on my Facebook page so that my clients and prospects get the same feel from all of my online communication. It's important to build a custom background for your page to really tie it in with your other online profiles and that's very easy to do online. There are a lot of different websites and companies that will build your background for you for a small fee ($5 on Fiverr.com), but I build mine for free through www.freetwitterdesigner.com. Just insert pictures, add text and then follow the instructions to load it onto your Twitter page. All of the instructions are in the free download at BestAgentIdeas.com. Just make sure you change the background position to "center" and you may need to click the "tile background" box in order to make it fit. Here is what my settings look like:

You can access the design of your Twitter page under the settings button, located in the upper right corner of the Twitter tool bar.

Twitter Basics

The biggest difference between Twitter and Facebook is that you only have 140 characters to say what you're going to say. That's a big change in communicating from the paragraphs you can write on your Facebook page. Twitter conversations are short and to the point. They have to be. This keeps the tone of Twitter conversations much more laid back and casual than Facebook. Twitter users value conversations and interaction and they use their own language. Let's take a look at the Twitter vocab:

Twitter Handle: Also known as a **username**. This is the name you select to represent yourself.

To Follow: To subscribe to someone's updates on Twitter. You do this by clicking the "Follow" button on that specific person's Twitter page, which can be found at **http://twitter.com/USERNAME**. (Insert the specific person's username into the URL, like http://twitter.com/MyInsuranceGuys). When you follow someone, their updates will be displayed on your Twitter page so you know what they are doing.

To Follow Back: To subscribe to the updates of someone who has recently started following you. Whenever a new person follows you, you receive an email alert from Twitter. In the email, there will be a link to that person's profile. By clicking the link, you can check out who they are and decide to follow them back or not. It is not required to follow everyone back, but many people like to.

Follower: A person who has subscribed to receive your updates. You can see your total number of followers on your Twitter profile page.

Update: Also known as a **tweet**. They can be no longer than 140-characters. *(Later we will talk about different types of updates.)* You post your update in the white text box under "What are you doing?"

@Reply: A public message sent from one Twitter user to another by putting **@USERNAME** at the beginning of the tweet.

Direct Message (or DM): A private message sent from one Twitter user to another by either clicking the "message" link on their profile or typing **D USERNAME**.

Twitter Stream: A list of a person's real-time updates. Every time you post an update, it goes into your Twitter stream, which is found on your account page also at **http://twitter.com/USERNAME**.

Tweet-up: An event specifically organized for Twitter-users to meet up and network, usually informal.

Hashtag (#): A tool to aggregate the conversation surrounding an event or theme; created by combining a # with a word, acronym or phrase (**#WORD**).

Retweet (or RT): To repeat what someone else has already tweeted. People do this if someone has said something especially valuable and they want their own network to see the information too. (Example: Retweet @USERNAME: Check out this cool resource).

Once you're signed up and you have your profile complete, it's time to put Twitter to work for your agency. The first step may seem a little counterintuitive but before you start tweeting, it's a good idea to follow and observe businesses similar to yours to see what they are doing well and learn from their mistakes. By following people, you will receive their updates on a regular basis in your Twitter stream. This is your chance to learn about their lives, check out the blog posts they are reading and meet the people they interact with. Following a good-sized community can be valuable and fun; it's also a big part of interacting with people on Twitter.

One of the neat things about Twitter is the ability to break down the people you follow into lists. You can have a list for your clients, your competitors, industry experts, industry organizations, local businesses, thought leaders, your prospects, etc. You don't need the permission of those you follow in order to receive their tweets and having the different lists of people you follow will allow you to see what your clients and prospects are up to as well as what your competition and industry experts are doing. You can create as many lists as you'd like and make them either public or private, depending on whether or not you want others to be able to see your lists. You can also add people to multiple lists. Keep in mind, users are notified when they are added to another user's list. Here is what my list looks like:

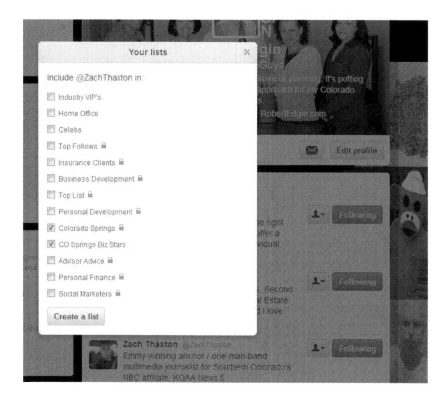

There are some other easy ways to find people to follow as well, including a few great websites like Twellow.com and search.twitter.com. They both allow you to enter search words like your city and then give you ideas as to who you may want to follow. Another great idea is to check and see who is being followed by your followers and those you follow. You can come across a lot of local people you may not have found otherwise. Once you're following someone, you have the ability to retweet (RT) something valuable that others have shared or direct message (DM) them to start a conversation.

What to Tweet

Just like posting on Facebook, "what the heck should I tweet about" is the most common question asked regarding Twitter. Most people think that you have to come up with a constant stream of funny, inspirational or life changing things to say, but that's just not true!

Does tweeting funny, inspirational or life changing things help you get more followers? Sure, but so does consistent tweeting about everything else - tips and tricks to keep your rates down, what's going on at your office, what's going on outside your office, etc. Plus, Twitter has an advantage over Facebook when it comes to content thanks to retweets. Retweeting is encouraged on Twitter, which means if you follow some great people then you'll always have things to share! All you have to do is find a tweet worth sharing, hover over it and then click the retweet button.

Twitter is a great place to drive traffic to everything else you do, especially your blog. When we get into chapter 16 and tie everything together in your social media plan, you'll see the importance of driving traffic to your blog in order to capture leads. Twitter is a great place to post a preview of a story in order to get people interested in reading the rest. It's simple and easy and looks like this:

Above, I've shared a link which leads to one of the articles I had previously posted on my blog. Remember, you only have 140 characters, so your tweet needs to be direct and to the point. Also, because of character constraints, you need to use a URL shortener when you are posting a link to a website. For example, the entire link to my blog article shared above is http://www.myinsuranceguysblog.com/2012/06/be-prepared-for-forest-fires.html, which is entirely too long to tweet. However, by using a URL shortener like www.tinyurl.com, you get a new, shorter link to copy and paste into your tweet. If you do your tweeting through Hootsuite, there is a built in tool to shorten a website link.

Mentioning your clients or prospects is still a great idea (just like it was when on Facebook), but when you do it in Twitter you need to put the @ symbol in front of their name so that they are alerted to the fact that someone mentioned them in a tweet. Even if they're not currently following you, it' a great idea to let your clients and prospects know you're thinking about them.

On a side note, most of the time when you mention someone they will start to follow you if they weren't already doing so. That's exactly what happened with the tweet above, where I thanked a client of mine for a book recommendation. Fifteen minutes later I had a new follower:

When planning out your week's tweets to coincide with your editorial calendar, it is helpful to have a theme for your tweets that you use each day of the week. This makes it easier to come up with content, photos and links to tweet and can also give your followers something to look forward to each week. Here is an example of a week's worth of themes:

1. Monday: Helpful tip or trick to start the week. Choose a tip that relates to your monthly topic from your editorial calendar, with a link to your blog for all of the information.
2. Tuesday: A behind the scenes look at your office. Take a photo of something going on at the office.
3. Wednesday: Link to a video that either you have previously recorded (we'll talk more about videos in chapter 12), or that relates to your monthly topic. You can find videos relating to anything and everything on Youtube.com.
4. Thursday: Link to an article or story written by someone else that relates to your monthly topic.
5. Friday: Picture or story about your people. Get a little more personal and give an interesting tidbit about someone in your office or one of your clients.
6. Saturday: Link to your blog. Post the headline of your monthly themed blog article with a link to the story.

In addition to these 6 tweets per week (or even better, multiples of these 6 tweets) tweet the random things that come up - funny things that happen, random acts of kindness, thanking your clients or referral sources, mentioning something a client has accomplished or retweeting an interesting story you come across. Before you know it and without much effort, you'll be the Twitter king or queen of your community.

Twitter Wrap Up

Remember to use Hootsuite or another similar program to make tweeting easier by combining all of your social media interactions into one place. You should also download the twitter app for your phone in case something comes up that's worth tweeting about while you're out and about. For example, if you're stopping by a coffee shop on the way home from work, send out a tweet offering to buy a latte for any of your clients that stop during a 15 minute window. Chances are that no one will show up, but you've done something important anyway. You've touched your clients in a way that they'll remember.

Everything we've discussed about Twitter is ultimately just another opportunity to touch your clients and prospects. Just like Facebook, you cannot control who sees each tweet, but for those that do, you'll quickly become the coolest insurance agent in town and build connections that will increase your retention, referrals and cross selling opportunities.

The last thing to discuss regarding Twitter is measuring your results and checking your Twitter reputation, both of which are easy to do. There are a lot of free sites that allow you to track your Twitter results, like www.twitonomy.com, which will graph your tweets, followers and more to give you an overview of your Twitter progress. You should also use the twitter search tool, search.twitter.com, to search for your name and your agency name to make sure you know about any negative conversations being had where your name is mentioned. Use the twitter search to find industry stories or people near you as well, it's a great tool.

Once you get involved with Twitter, you'll find it can actually be kind of fun. It's easier to use than Facebook and, although it doesn't have as many users, it provides more immediate and straightforward access to stories, links and photos. It's a great way to share what you've got going on and it's a great addition to your 21st Century Communication plan.

YOUR BLOG

There are quite a few technical definitions for the word blog. The dictionary defines a blog as "a web site containing the writer's or group of writer's own experiences, observations, opinions, etc. and often having images and links to other web sites." Harvard law defines it as "a hierarchy of text, images, media objects and data, arranged chronologically, that can be viewed in an HTML browser" and according to Wikipedia, a blog is "a discussion or informational site published on the world wide web and consisting of discreet entries ("posts") typically displayed in reverse chronological order (the most recent post appears first).

A blog is technically all of those things listed above, but YOUR blog is so much more. The above definitions describe what a blog does but they miss out on what a blog can mean for your agency and do for your agency. Your blog is the center of your 21st Century Communication universe. If this were Star Wars, your blog would be the Death Star, traveling the web (and your town) and blowing your competition off the map. Your blog has an immense amount of power because you own it and you control it. No one can tell you what you have to do or say on your blog (with the exception of your compliance department, of course). You make the rules for your blog. Additionally, if you can get people to your blog, you have NO competition for your client's and prospects attention.

Your blog is where all of your other communication leads people. All of your other 21st Century Communication tools are yellow brick roads that take people to Oz - your blog! If it sounds like I'm making a really big deal about you having a blog, you're absolutely right. When used properly, a blog will provide you and your agency with tremendous opportunities. Your blog is a great way to provide value to your clients and prospects by sharing information that they need and want. It's a great place to show your expertise and knowledge. You can discuss products and cases in an educational way that clients can relate to which allows you to sell without having to do any selling. Your blog will produce leads that ask you to sell them something AND tell you what it is they want you to sell them. Your blog will set you apart from most other agents in town and highlight you as what you really are; an expert and the best choice as agent and advisor in your town.

One quick story should illustrate the potential and power of your blog. I recently received a call from Leslie. Leslie is a friend of a friend to my wife on Facebook. About 18 months ago, my wife shared a link to a blog post that I had written on her Facebook page. Her friend on Facebook saw the link, read the post and then "liked" it on Facebook. Her friend's friend did the same thing which added a link to my blog on Leslie's Facebook page (a testament to the power of Facebook, but not the point of the story). According to Leslie, my blog soon became her source of information for all things insurance. Around that same time, Leslie had tried calling her insurance agent about a problem she was having but felt that he was unconvincing in his answer and annoyed that she had called. Luckily, she found the answer on my blog.

For the past 18 months, she would check back with my blog for information or to see what new posts I had written. Eventually, she decided to call my office so we could talk. Although she lives an hour and a half away from my office, she was requesting an appointment so we could sit down and review her family's insurance and financial situation. I assured her there were agents much closer to her, including a few that worked for the same company as me, that I could introduce her to. Her answer to that suggestion was fantastic. "I've been getting all of my information from you and getting to know you for the past 18 months through your blog and your Facebook page. Why would I want to work with anyone else?" How could I argue with that?

How to Set Up Your Blog

Okay, you're convinced that you need a blog, now you just need to go out and do it. There are plenty of highly technical, very expensive platforms out there for running your own blog. However, there are also plenty of ways to run your blog with NO techie skills needed and NO money out of pocket required and that's what we're going to concentrate on. The best site on the web for beginning bloggers is blogger.com. Blogger.com is a part of the Google family of products and is designed to be extremely simple for anyone and everyone to launch a blog. There is no charge to set up your blog, other than buying your domain name if you want one - which all the smart people do.

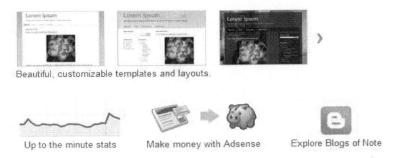

Once you log in or create your free account, creating a blog is as simple as clicking the "New Blog" button. When you do, a box pops up with a few important decisions to make.

The first decision is the title of your blog. If you're as smart as I think you are, you'll choose a name that matches up with everything else you do in your 21st Century Communication plan. For example, on Facebook and Twitter I go by MyInsuranceGuys, so the name of my blog is…you guessed it, My Insurance Guys Blog and the address where it can be found is www.MyInsuranceGuysBlog.com - simple enough.

The next decision to make is the address of your blog. You have two options, either use the name that is assigned by blogger, which will be the title of your blog @blogspot.com or you can add a custom domain name. Both options work but I would really recommend getting a custom name for marketing purposes. MyInsuranceGuysBlog.com sounds a whole lot better and will give you a much more professional look than MyInsuranceGuysBlog@blogspot.com. You can get your custom domain name through blogger or any other domain service, like Go Daddy.

The third and final decision is the layout of your blog. There are a lot of different styles to choose from and I'm sure there's at least one of them that will appeal to you. Don't worry about picking one that you don't like. You can change the look of your blog at any time by clicking the layout button in the left tool bar and then clicking template designer button (located near the top right of the page). That's it! Your blog is now ready for you to start adding content and spreading it around for your clients, prospects and everyone else in your city to see!

Writing Tips for Your Blog Posts

Everyone thinks that writing articles for your blog is the hardest part, which is good news for you because it keeps most agents from ever trying. The truth is, writing a blog is as easy as talking to your favorite client and that's exactly how each post should come across. A blog post is really just your thoughts and opinions in written form. There's no reason to treat a blog post as if you're writing a formal paper for your English class. In fact, blogs work a heck of a lot better when you write as if you were speaking, using your own voice and letting your personality shine through.

The best way for people to get to know you through your blog is to be true to yourself and your personality. Don't try to change who you are or be something you're not just because you're writing to someone instead of talking to them. In fact, a great tip when writing is to pretend as if you are actually speaking to one of your favorite clients. As you talk to them (in your mind) about a certain subject, type out what you're saying. If you need to, you can even buy a speech to text program that will type out your conversations for you. Your clients should be able to read each article and know it was written by you.

Your blog posts should be relatively short, 300 - 600 words, so you don't have to worry about coming up with a 5 page paper. In fact, once you start writing, you'll find it's harder to keep your articles short than it is to add too much and make them long. If you're writing about something that is going to need more than 600 words, break it up into multiple posts. This idea works great with your editorial calendar so that you can have subtopics to add throughout the month about monthly topic.

Make sure you use a compelling headline for each blog post. I can't overstress how important this is. The headline must grab your reader's attention and get them to want to read the actual article. The headline is the most read part of any article or post (8 out of 10 people will read the headline) so it has to be appealing enough to make your reader want more (only 2 out of 10 people will read the article). If your headline isn't appealing, most readers will think that the article won't be appealing either. Start each post with the headline in mind and come up with a great headline before writing your article. Then re-write 10 more similar headlines so you have a number of them to choose from after finishing your article. Here are some tips for coming up with catchy headlines:

1. Use numbers: the next time you're at the grocery store, look at how many magazine articles at the checkout counter use numbers in the headline.
2. Use interesting adjectives: People like to read things that sound fascinating or interesting (two good examples of interesting adjectives). Here are some examples:
    a. Effortless
    b. Free
    c. Absolute
    d. Incredible
    e. Strange
3. Use trigger words like what, why, how and when.
4. Create a swipe file: a swipe file is a collection of great headlines that you can cheat off of anytime you need a little help or inspiration. To help you get started with your swipe file, I've got a list of the **top 100 headlines of all times** that you can download for free. Just go to www.BestAgentIdeas.com and click on "Book Owners".

Make sure you include a visual element in your blog posts as well. The first thing people look at when reading something may be your headline, but the 2nd and 3rd most looked at part of all articles are the pictures and the photo's caption. Add a photo to every blog and then use the space under the photo to add something that you want to make sure your readers pay attention to. The age old saying, "A picture is worth a thousand words" is still true today.

Don't forget to use your spell check and grammar check before publishing your blog posts. I try to type what I'm speaking, which means I'm usually trying to type pretty fast. Throw in the fact that I peck type (2 fingers and a thumb) without looking at the screen (I have to watch the keyboard) and what you get is a story or post full of spelling and grammar errors. Fortunately, most programs are pretty adept at catching almost every error you can come up with so you publish your posts error free. In addition to using your spell check, I'd also recommend using your "spouse check." I email every post to my wife, who happens to be a much better grammar analyst than me, for a final spot check. Find someone who is willing to take 5 minutes and do a quick review of your work before you make it public for the world to see.

Finding Topics for Your Blog Posts

I happen to enjoy writing but I know not everyone does. Don't worry, writing for your blog is nothing like writing the papers you used to have to turn in for grades back in school. Blog posts don't have to be formal, they don't have to be perfectly punctuated, they don't have to contain a beginning, middle and end, and they don't have to be very long. A blog post is YOUR opinion or YOUR thoughts in written form, nothing more. If you can speak, which you probably do a lot of all day, every day at the office, then you can write a post for your blog. At first, it may take you 60 to 90 minutes to write a blog post, but once you do it a few times and get a little practice in you'll be writing posts in 15 - 20 minutes. Every post gets easier, especially if you are writing about a topic you know a great deal about. Here are some ideas to get you going:

You actually write multiple blog posts in your head every single day when you're talking to your clients. Every conversation with a client regarding their coverage is a blog post waiting to be written down. Your client's questions are a great place to start collecting topics for your blog posts. Most clients have the same questions about coverage and billing and types of policies, all you need to do is keep a pad of paper next to your phone and write down the questions as they come in. Within the course of a week you'll have 25 questions written down that can be answered on your blog.

Run through a personal insurance review (PIR) and you've got a dozen more blog posts ideas. What is this coverage? Why do you need that endorsement? Which deductible is right for you? Do you have the correct replacement cost estimate for your home or is it underinsured? Are you getting all of the discounts you deserve? Are your liability limits high enough? Are they too high? Do you have coverage you don't need? Why are your rates going up? What's credit got to do with your insurance price? The list goes on and on. Record yourself answering the questions or going through a mock PIR and you'll have you're blog posts already written out. You just need to transcribe what you say in the recordings.

Tell personal stories about yourself, your family or a situation that you've been in that relates to insurance. Remember, you want your clients and prospects to get to know you and your personality through your blog. Blog posts about you or something you've been involved in give people an inside look at who you really are. Besides, people love stories and enjoy them a lot more than an informational or educational blog post. If you can share something in story form your clients and prospects will read more of it and remember more of it. Tell stories whenever possible.

My Insurance Guys Blog

protect your assets. preserve your lifestyle. prepare for your future.

| My Insurance Guy's Blog | Wildfire Ready | Know Your Retirement Number |

MONDAY, FEBRUARY 4, 2013

Broken Legs, Skier's Liability, And Your Home Insurance Policy

Ski season is in full effect, and Colorado ski resorts are finally getting some much needed snow. My son and I decided to take advantage of the fresh powder and headed west, along with what seemed to be half of the residents of Colorado, for a day of fun in the snow. But unfortunately, I was involved in a very serious collision with a 6 year old boy that resulted in a broken leg and a trip to the hospital...for the little boy.

While skiing down an advanced run, I looked up the mountain to see if it was safe to make my way across. As I looked up, I saw Colton (named changed) coming at me at a very high rate of speed. Colton wasn't out of control, but he was going too fast and was not able to turn very well yet (which is why he was coming straight down the mountain). There was nowhere for me to go so I braced for impact and did my best to catch Colton as we collided in order to, hopefully, prevent serious injuries. Fortunately, Colton and I were both wearing helmets and, fortunately, I was able to wrap Colton up in my arms and fall in a way that put most of the impact on me. Unfortunately, Colton's leg landed under me and, as we slid down the slope, his leg was broken.

It's okay to lighten things up every once in a while too. Not every post has to be serious or even teach people anything. You can profile a client's business and share community information; you can talk about your vacation or even do a review of a new restaurant. As long as you're writing and sharing something then you're doing what's important, touching your clients. You're giving them a reminder of who you are, what you do, the products you sell and all of the great things about you that make them like you so much. Even the posts that your clients choose not to read have an impact on your relationship because it makes you look more professional.

My Insurance Guy's Blog	Wildfire Ready	Know Your Retirement Number

WEDNESDAY, AUGUST 29, 2012

A Review: Crave Burger

What does a "3 Little Pigs" burger from Crave Burgers have to do with insurance? Absolutely nothing! But, since I've been focuing on "A Taste Of Colorado" throughout the year and giving away gift cards to Colorado based restaurants, it seemed like a good excuse to indulge in one of my favorite guilty pleasures, a cheeseburger!

However, calling the "3 Little Pigs" a cheeseburger is kind of like saying the Mona Lisa is "just a painting." As far as cheeseburgers go, this is more of a masterpiece! For starters, it's made from scratch when I order so it was super fresh. Not only is it fresh, I can tell by looking at my burger that the ingredients are all top quality.

Speaking of the ingredients, as the name implies the "3 Little Pigs" burger is topped with 3 different, yet equally delicious, types of pork. PLUS, they piled a mound of onion strings in top too (my mouth is watering again just writing about it!). Even the bun was awesome.

The burger itself is bigger than my mouth , super juicy and super tasty. My plan was to cut it in 1/2 and save the other 1/2 for dinner but I wasn't ready to quit eating after I made it through the first 1/2 so I ended up eating the whole thing. I will, however, be skipping dinner!

Here are some more ideas for blog topics:

1. Answer client's questions
2. Debunk an insurance myth (red cars cost more to insure)

3. Profile a client
4. Pay attention to news stories and give your opinion. MSN and AOL run stories all of the time that are great for blog posts (see MSN home page article on next page)
5. Create a "how to" tutorial.
6. Write "5 things you didn't know about..." posts
7. Review events you've attended
8. Give your short opinion about a story and then link to the actual story
9. Present client case studies (a great way to teach people something)
10. Provide a review and a link to a useful tool or app
11. Write "Top ___ reasons why you should (or should not)..." posts
12. Write "How I use..." posts
13. Review books you've read
14. Compare and contrast different products or coverage
15. Use top ten lists
16. Check other insurance blogs for topics
17. Highlight a staff member
18. Give a behind the scenes office tour or updates about office happenings
19. Give the highlights of your family vacation
20. Discuss your hobbies
21. Set up a Google alert with search topics that you can share through your blog. To find Google alerts, just do a Google search for Google alerts

There are plenty of other ideas for content, you just need to use a little creativity and be true to who you are. Write about the things you find interesting and the things you talk about every day and you'll never run out of topics.

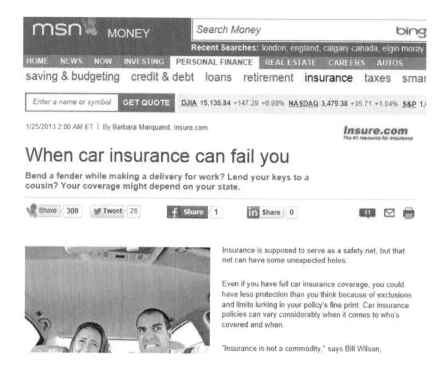

1/25/2013 2:00 AM ET | By Barbara Marquand, insure.com

Insure.com
The #1 resource for insurance

When car insurance can fail you

Bend a fender while making a delivery for work? Lend your keys to a cousin? Your coverage might depend on your state.

Insurance is supposed to serve as a safety net, but that net can have some unexpected holes.

Even if you have full car insurance coverage, you could have less protection than you think because of exclusions and limits lurking in your policy's fine print. Car insurance policies can vary considerably when it comes to who's covered and when.

"Insurance is not a commodity," says Bill Wilson,

Now That the Writing is Over, The real Work Begins

If this were "Field of Dreams", I'd tell you that if you write it, they will come, but unfortunately, that's just not true. It does not matter how good your blog posts are, no one is going to see them unless you do a little bit of work to get them seen. Plus, if you don't get your blog seen it will do nothing to help you retain your clients or grow your agency. I'll be honest, getting your blog seen actually takes more work than writing the blog. Your blog has to compete with all other media and distractions for your clients' and prospects' attention, which can be a challenge. However, there are some tried and true tactics to get your posts read and your clients and prospects involved.

When you finish a blog post, Blogger gives you the opportunity to add tags or labels. This is what Google uses to help people find your blog posts. When someone goes to Google to search for something, your blog may show up for them to look at if Google feels it is relevant to the person's search. Don't get too excited, it will take time for Google to start recommending your blog to people because it needs to become "aged" before Google will even acknowledge that it exists. If anyone ever finds your blog on their own, consider it a bonus. Most of the people reading your blog will be directed there by you and from your own personal efforts, but that's okay, because those are really the only people that matter anyway. Your blog is an amazing tool to help solidify client relationships and prove your worth to new prospects, so those are the only people you need to make sure see your blog.

Everything you do in your agency's 21ˢᵗ Century Communication plan should lead people to your blog. We already talked about one of the why's (Google Juice) and we'll talk about the other big why in a moment (your call to action), but the good news is that when everything you do leads to your blog, it gives your blog a lot of momentum. Here are some specific places to add your blog address to and some strategies you can use in order to get you blog seen:

1. Add a link to your email signature
2. Give the headline and a link to the post in Facebook
3. Tweet it
4. Put it on your business card
5. Make specific business cards just for your blog
6. Start a story in your newsletter and direct people to your blog for the rest of the story
7. Make videos in YouTube that relate to a blog story and link to your blog
8. When a client emails you a question, respond by sending them a link to a blog post you've written that contains the answer (and gives them more information about the topic they didn't even think to ask)
9. Make a sticker with the address and use it to seal your office envelopes
10. Email blog articles to prospects as part of your follow up process
11. Put the link anywhere and everywhere!

Over time, your blog somewhat takes on a life of its own. You still have to provide the content and moderate the posts, but somehow it starts to spread across the internet and be seen without you helping it. It takes time and a commitment to posting on a regular basis (try to post a couple of blogs per month) but it does happen. It's kind of magical to watch and Blogger makes it easy for you to track your results and see how your blog is doing through their easy to understand analytics.

My Insurance Guys Blog · Stats › Overview   Jul 4, 2013 10:00 AM – Jul 11, 2013 9:00 AM   C   Now   D

Pageviews today	51
Pageviews yesterday	47
Pageviews last month	854
Pageviews all time history	22,183
Don't track your own pageviews	

More »

Posts

Entry	Pageviews
Renting a Moving Truck - What Kin... Mar 11, 2010, 3 comments	24
What If My Insurance Company Do... Mar 28, 2010, 2 comments	20
8 Links to Keep You Safe on Color... Nov 15, 2009	11
Colorado Hail Season Is About To ... May 17, 2012	7
Home Insurance Guest Medical Co... Oct 22, 2012	6

Traffic Sources

Entry	Pageviews
http://myinsuranceguys.blogspot.c...	26
https://www.google.com/	6
http://www.google.com/search?biw...	2

Audience

More »

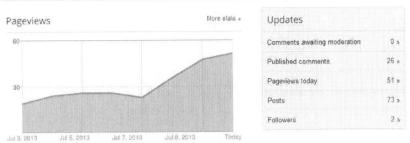

My Insurance Guys Blog · Overview

Pageviews — Top traffic sources - myinsuranceguys.blogspot.com | www.google.com | myinsuranceguys.blogspot.co.uk

Updates

Comments awaiting moderation	0 »
Published comments	26 »
Pageviews today	51 »
Posts	73 »
Followers	2 »

From the 2 charts above, you can see that I've had 22,183 page views of my blog as of the day I'm writing this, 854 in the last month alone, 51 so far this morning (9:30 AM). You can also see which posts are being looked at this morning and where the people (traffic) are coming from. If you want even more information, you can scroll down for more detailed views. By clicking into the "Traffic Sources", I can see how people are finding my blog.

My Insurance Guys Blog · Stats › Traffic sources   Jun 11, 2013 – Jul 10, 2013

Referring URLs

Entry	Pageviews
http://myinsuranceguys.blogspot.c...	112
https://www.google.com/	34
http://myinsuranceguys.blogspot.c...	9
http://myinsuranceguys.blogspot.jp/	7
http://www.google.com/	5
http://blogs.needz.it	4
http://myinsuranceguys.blogspot.com	4
http://myinsuranceguys.blogspot.c...	3
http://www.google.com	3
http://www.google.com.ph/search?...	3

Referring Sites

Entry	Pageviews
myinsuranceguys.blogspot.com	125
www.google.com	90
myinsuranceguys.blogspot.co.uk	9
www.google.co.uk	8
myinsuranceguys.blogspot.jp	7
www.bing.com	7
www.google.ca	6
search.yahoo.com	5

When you first get your blog going, you may be better off not even looking at the statistics for your blog as they can be somewhat discouraging. Instead, focus on delivering quality content to quality people. Just like your number of "likes" on Facebook or your followers on Twitter, quality really does trump quantity when it comes to the people who read your blog posts. If you get the right posts in front of the right people, your blog will produce amazing results. It will remind your clients of how good you are, show your prospects how much better you are and will bring leads right to your doorstep!

Capturing Leads - The REAL Power of Your Blog

Because you have complete control of your blog and you're in a competitive vacuum when people are reading your blog (there are no ads for your competition on your blog competing for your client's attention) it is a great place to capture leads - especially for cross-selling your clients. The ability to capture leads is THE main reason you want all of your other 21st Century Communication tools leading people to your blog. Think about this for a minute. If someone takes the time to read 300 - 600 words about a specific topic on your blog, they're probably pretty interested in that topic, at least momentarily. It is the perfect opportunity to capture a lead by offering the reader more information about the topic through a video, report or other irresistible offer.

Every blog post you write should give the reader the opportunity to raise their hand and request more information. When they do, you've got someone to talk to who has a problem or situation they need help with. If you had 5, 10, 15 or 20 people a month raising their hands and asking you to give them more information to help them solve a problem, do you think you would make more sales? Even if you didn't sell something, if you were providing valuable information to your clients instead of them getting it from another source (a different insurance agent or advisor) do you think your client retention would go up? Absolutely!

The key is including an irresistible offer and a strong call to action that will make your clients or prospects raise their hand and request more information. There are entire books and courses dedicated to the art of writing irresistible offers and good calls to action and the small amount of space I have available here to discuss the subject is not going to be enough to give you what you need to become a pro at either. However, there are a few rules to follow that will help you get started. I'll also give you some more resources so that you can devote as much time as you'd like to the art of writing an irresistible offer and call to action. Keep in mind as you begin the process, any offer (even if it's not irresistible) will provide better results than NO offer and no offer is what you and every other agent in town has been making. In other words, don't worry about waiting for your offers to be perfect before you start the process of capturing leads. Done and in use always produces better results than almost perfect but not in use. You can always go back and change an offer into something better later.

Your irresistible offer should be tied to the subject of the blog post that your clients are reading and offer them some additional or expanded information on the same subject. For example, if you're writing a post about not naming under-age children as your beneficiary, your irresistible offer should be for **more** information relating to beneficiaries and not something else, like the best method to choosing the right amount of life insurance coverage. An even better choice would be to offer a report on "The 5 people to consider as your beneficiary and the 3 people you should NEVER name as your beneficiary." Another idea would be for a special paper on "What to do if you want your under-age children to be your life insurance beneficiary."

Every time you write an article or blog post, stop and think about what the people reading the post really want. Why are they reading the article and what do they hope to learn or achieve? The two biggest motivators in life are fear and greed. Notice I did not say that fear and greed are the only motivators, but they are the biggest. What can you offer as a follow up to your post that will either alleviate your reader's pain or satisfy their desire? If your offer can do one of these two things, there's a good chance your reader will raise their hand and request the information.

Use **power words** whenever possible in your irresistible offer and call to action. The 5 most powerful words in the English language (at least according to marketers) are:

1. You (the only thing better is using someone's name)
2. Free
3. Because (when asking people to do something, they are for more likely to do it if there is a reason. For example, "you need to get the report I'm offering **because**...)
4. Instantly (people don't like to wait for information)
5. New

Some other word tricks include using numbers (4 out of 5..., 100% improvement..., 10 reasons why...), starting your offer and call to action with a subject or verb and using adverbs sparingly.

Make the outcome of your offer plain to see. What, EXACTLY, will your client or prospect gain by accepting your free offer? What will they

117

learn? What will they be able to do? What will they be able to STOP doing? People really want to know what they are going to get out of your free report or video or meeting before they raise their hand to get it. Unfortunately, our society has become so negative and untrusting toward offers of any kind and they are so used to telling people "no" that they need plenty of good reasons to say "yes". One of the power words that can help overcome this is "because". "This report is being offered to you free of charge **because** I want all of my clients to know how to…"

Provide social proof that your offer is worthwhile whenever you possibly can. This is where testimonials come in and do wonders for your marketing. Reviews and testimonials - things that others say about you - are always more powerful than anything you can say about yourself. I don't have the space to discuss a testimonial program, but if you don't yet have one, add it to your list of things to do.

Once you make your irresistible offer, your CALL TO ACTION (CTA) is what gets your client or prospect to actually take action and raise their hand for more information. A call to action is short, easy and direct. Your CTA is the box that says "Click Here" or the direction to "Call the Office" or "Email Me for Your Free…" Keep in mind that the less you require of people in your CTA, the more people will choose to take you up on your offer. If you only require that people enter their first name and email in order to get something, you'll get more people than if you require first name, last name, phone number and email. And you'll get more people asking for those 4 things than you will if you're also asking for their address, date of birth, etc. Only ask for the minimum amount of information needed from your client or prospect in order to get them the information they requested. If you are physically mailing something, they'll understand that you need their address, but if you're emailing a report or some other item, you need a lot less. I like to ask for their first name, last name and email address and that is it. Here is a sample of an irresistible offer and CTA.

You see other people's offers and calls to action hundreds of times per day online, on TV and you even hear them on the radio. Start paying attention to the ones that make you want to click or call in and model your own offers and CTA's after the successful ads you come across. Here are a few I came across today while I was in the process of writing this chapter:

Things to Offer as Your Irresistible Offer

By now you're probably thinking great, I can put together an irresistible offer, but what the heck am I supposed to be offering people? If the idea of coming up with a bunch of great reports, guides or books that people will raise their hand and request sounds like work, you're absolutely right! However, just because you're offering a free piece of information does not mean it has to be YOUR free piece of information. I develop quite a few of my guides, reports and other pieces of information, but it is NOT something that you have to do. There are plenty of resources you can offer that have been developed and put together by other experts that are just as valuable to your client (or perhaps more) than anything you could develop on your own.

For example, I recently offered two free reports on preparing for the upcoming wildfire season and protecting your home and family from wildfires (a big topic of interest in Colorado these days). Also included with the free report was all of the information needed to qualify for a $2,500 tax credit for fire mitigation performed on your property. The information included a wildfire home assessment and checklist along with tons of great tips for protecting your home and family. All in all, the report was 54 pages long. How much of it did I develop? None! The reports were put together by the Insurance Institute for Business and Home Safety, the Firewise Community Fire Prevention Partnership and the State of Colorado.

All of the reports were online and free for consumers to download and use IF they were out searching the web for the info and IF they happened to come across the free reports. However, most people didn't know they should be looking for the information to begin with until I brought it to their attention (through my blog, newsletter and other marketing) and pointed out all of the good reasons to prepare for wildfires. On a side not, the free report was offered one month before the costliest and most devastating wildfire in Colorado history, the Black Forest Fire, which destroyed close to 500 homes and resulted in more than 3,600 insurance claims!

Did you know you may qualify for a $2500 tax credit for mitigating the fire risk around your home? Depending on where you live, you may be able to take advantage of a tax credit that expires at the end of 2013 which helps offset the cost or protecting your home from wildfire!

To help make sure your home is wildfire ready AND you get any type of tax credit you may qualify for, we've gathered up all of the information into one great report! Input your information below for an instant download.

First Name *

Last Name *

Email *

Phone 1

Submit

If you take a few minutes and search Google for the topic you are writing a post about, you can often find PDF's of full reports that are available for download. You should never try to pass the reports off as your own but you can definitely pass the information on to your clients and prospects if the information is free on the web and goes along with your message. It's important (and professional) to make sure you give proper credit to the author.

There are plenty of other great sources for your irresistible offer(s) that will require little or no work on your part, some of them include:

1. A chapter (or part of a chapter) from a book about your topic. For example, I often offer information from books written by well-known financial gurus that coincide with a particular blog post.
2. The entire book! You can often buy books in bulk at a price low enough to offer an entire book to your client or prospect. I've bought cases of the "Tax Free Retirement" book by Patrick Kelly, as well as, the "Paychecks and Playchecks" book by Tom Hegna to give away to my clients.
3. EzineArticles.com, which is a great source for free content designed for newsletters, offers hundreds of thousands of articles ready to be shared.
4. Links to information: sometimes you don't even need a report, you can just gather up a bunch of useful links about your topic and offer them up in one place. This is exactly what I did in the "Know Your Number" offer that I made.
5. Checklists: People LOVE checklists because they know that someone has gone through the trouble of listing out the things that need to be done and a way to measure whether they are done or not. More times than not, you can find downloadable checklists with a few searches on the web.
   a. Just typing the words "insurance checklist" into Google produces 28,800,000 results in 0.12 seconds!
6. Buy them: there are plenty of people and organizations who are willing to share the reports they've put together for a small fee. **Shameless plug: you can find some great reports available for purchase at www.BestAgentIdeas.com!

Capturing Leads With Your CTA

Once people raise their hand because of your irresistible offer, you need to determine how they will request it. What does your CTA want them to do in order to get the information or report you are offering? In other words, you need to determine how you are going to capture that lead. You have a lot of choices. You can make them call you, they can email you or you could make them stop by the office and pick it up. I typically use software that allows people to enter their name and email (or whatever else I decide is required) and then click the "Get Report" button in order to access the information immediately.

While there are plenty of options when it comes to how people will request your information, some definitely work better than others. In general, the more someone has to do to get your information, the less they will request it. More of their personal information being required will result in fewer requests, but this is not always a bad thing. You may be offering a $20 book that you don't want to spend a fortune on buying so you require a phone call to reserve their copy and a trip to the office to pick it up (because there is a limited quantity, the offer may be perceived as more valuable and help drive people to request it). You may want people to email you a survey or questionnaire if what you are offering requires some additional information for a specialized report (like an "income replacement analysis" or a "lawsuit protection analysis").

It is important to have a few systems or programs in place that will allow you to capture people's information in an easy way and, more importantly, allow them to provide it in an easy way. You should consider buying a dummy phone number with a voicemail box in order to allow people to "leave your name and email address in our report line voice mail so we can email you you're valuable report." With a little bit of work you can build forms that are stored in Google Drive that allow people to answer questions and then have the form sent to you. You can also build specific pages on your blog and then enter a contact box for people to enter their information. Both of those options will require you to do some work, which you can avoid if you're willing to spend a little bit of money.

There are companies out there, such as UnBounce, Hubspot and Sales Fusion, that will sell you everything you need to capture leads with prices ranging from not too much to way too much. Your best bet is to start off with something that will be easy on you until you really get into the report and lead capture groove. If you require someone to email you or call your dedicated number, you may get less leads but it will still be more leads than you are capturing now and you won't get overwhelmed in the set up process. Remember, something good and in use performs way better than something that is almost perfect but not in use. Just give your clients and prospects some way, or two ways, to raise their hand and request the information and you'll be on the right track. You can add in more sophistication later.

123

Blog Wrap Up

While a blog is not the end all, be all of your 21st Century Communication plan, it should play a major role because of the ability to communicate with your clients and prospects in a competitive vacuum AND the amazing potential your blog has to capture leads. Blogs are easy to set up, easy to maintain and easy to fill up with posts. Remember to keep a pad of paper next to your office phone so you write down your client's questions and start compiling a list of questions to answer in your blog. Every post you write will get easier than the one before it and before you know it you'll be creating posts in 15 - 20 minutes.

Promoting your blog to your clients and prospects is vitally important because *it doesn't matter how good your blog is if no one sees it!* Do everything you can to start directing clients to your blog on a regular basis. Make sure your posts give your clients and prospects an opportunity to raise their hand and request more information on the topic. Use free reports and a good call to action to capture their name and email address. Make it as easy as possible for them to ask for the info and then follow up with them afterword to take care of their need. Even if your offer doesn't lead to a sale, you can bet it will lead to higher retention, more satisfied clients and more referrals!

YOUTUBE - A VIDEO REVOLUTION

More than 1 billion visitors watch over 3 billion videos every day, a total of 6 billion hours of video every single month, on YouTube. YouTube is watched by more 18 - 34 year olds than any cable network and, after Google, YouTube is the second most used search engine in the world (6). In other words, YouTube is very, very popular and for a good reason! How many people would rather watch something than read something? If a picture is worth a thousand words, how much is a video worth? More people learn through seeing and hearing than they do by reading so leaving video out of your marketing and retention plan means you are not appealing to how the majority of people want to learn new things.

If you're going to implement a 21st Century Communication plan, there are no good excuses for not making videos for your clients and prospects. There are some bad excuses:

- It's too hard: Not true! YouTube makes it very easy to create, upload, edit and share your videos
- It's expensive to get the camera equipment: Wrong! 90% of the people who read this book will already have the equipment needed - a webcam or phone with video
- You have a face for radio: Okay, there's not much I can do for you on this one but it doesn't matter! You are who you are and you look how you look. Clients and prospects are going to see you in real life. You might as well prepare them for how you look through video. Besides, you're not trying to be a national celebrity or award winning actor and, more than likely, no one will see your videos unless you personally give them the link.
- You don't know what to say: Incorrect! Talking is easier than typing and you're probably pretty good at it or you wouldn't be in the insurance business. You just need to get used to seeing yourself do it.
- You don't speak well: No one cares! One of the great things

125

about YouTube is that clients and prospects get to see the real you. No one is perfect and you don't need to try to be for your client and prospect videos. Just like video mail, YouTube allows your personality to shine through when you're communicating.

- You don't know how: We're going to fix that.

It's important to give people as many different styles of communication as possible when reaching out to them because you never know which of your clients responds best to which type of media. If you send out a ton of great articles to a new prospect who hates to read, your good content and good intentions don't get you anywhere, and none of the bad excuses you can come up with to not use video outweigh that fact.

For better or for worse, the majority of the videos you make will ONLY be seen people who receive a specific link to the video by you. In fact, you don't even have to make your videos public if you don't want to. They can be classified as private and only be seen by a select group of people or as unlisted, in which case you must have a direct link in order to find the video. Even if your videos are listed as public they will probably never go viral and never be seen by ½ the world's population, it just doesn't work that way. However, if you ever want a shot at your blog, website or agency becoming famous (either in your hometown or across the world) you've got to add video to the equation and YouTube is your best choice.

YouTube is owned by Google so when people do Google searches for a specific subject, YouTube videos pull well and show up. You're given 15 whole minutes for each video, which is plenty of time (too much in fact), to make videos about any subject you want to discuss with clients and prospects. If you're going to make a video that is close to 15 minutes long, consider breaking down the subject into two or 3 videos at 3 - 5 minutes each so people won't get bored while watching them. The nice thing about video as a communication tool is that it allows clients and prospects to really see your personality. I'm not saying you have to have a great personality in order to use video, I'm saying that whatever personality type you have will shine through on your videos and that's a good thing. If people are going to do business with you for any extended amount of time, a big part of the reason is that they like your personality, so there's no reason to hide it by avoiding video.

The Best Way to Use YouTube

You may be wondering why you need to use YouTube with clients and prospects if you are already sending them video mail (discussed in chapter 13). Think about it this way: your video mail is a personal communication from you to a specific person. Your YouTube communication is more like a reference library or learning center. YouTube is not a piece personal communication; it's a mini TV show that teaches your clients or prospects something. It's a great way to stay in touch in a non-selling, non-threatening way while still educating people about what you do and what they should buy.

There are a few ways to really shine with your YouTube account and grow your agency, especially when dealing with new clients or prospects. Unfortunately, not every prospect is going to become a client the first time you talk to them. Some relationships take years to develop but the majority of agents have NO system in place to keep the communication going until the time is right to convert a prospect into a client (a topic that could easily fill up another book!). Remember, people buy when they are ready to buy, not when you are ready to sell, so it is important to have a follow up plan in place to convert cold prospects into hot leads and hot leads into new clients. The average sale takes 8 "no's" to get to a "yes", but most agents don't have a system in place to work through those 8 "no's". YouTube should be a big part of your prospect drip system (a consistent, ongoing set of messages that drip on the prospect at regular times) because it is a very non-threatening way to stay in front of prospects, display your professionalism and expertise. Most importantly, it lets them get to know you and become familiar with you.

In science, the **mere-exposure effect** is a psychological phenomenon in which people tend to develop a preference for things merely because they are familiar with them. In studies of interpersonal attraction, the more often a person is seen by someone, the more pleasing, likeable and intelligent that person appears to be. In social psychology, this is sometimes called the **familiarity principle**. In other words, having a follow up system that includes video for a prospect that didn't buy will make you more pleasing and likeable to the prospect so that the next time they are in a buying mode you have a better chance at making the sale. All things being equal, people choose to do business with someone they know, like and trust. All things being unequal, people STILL choose to do business with someone they know, like and trust. Your YouTube videos will help your prospects know, like and trust you!

The same principle is true for clients that are new to your agency. You've made the sale, which is a great start. Now, it's time to start solidifying the relationship and preparing your new client a long-term relationship, cross-sales and referrals. A YouTube video library as a part of your new client campaign will allow them to become much more familiar with you in a shorter amount of time so that they feel like they know, like and trust you and want to keep doing business with you. It's also a great way to introduce your new clients to other things you offer in your agency without coming across as a pushy salesman.

Setting Up YouTube and Creating Videos

YouTube is completely free and easy to both set up and use. You'll need a Google account to use YouTube, so if you did not create one for your blog yet, now is the time to get it done. If you already have a Google account, you have a YouTube account too, simply login with your Google account credentials.

First things first, make your YouTube channel name match the name of everything else you've done so far. My blog, Facebook, Twitter and YouTube channel are all called My Insurance Guys. Also, just like everything else you've set up so far, YouTube needs the profile to be completely filled out. Think of it as free advertising space and don't let it go to waste. Fortunately, YouTube has a great checklist up at the top of your home page so you know what has been, and still needs to be, done. To get to your home page, look at the left tool bar underneath the YouTube logo and you will see your screen name followed by "Watch Later", "Watch History" and "Playlists." Click on your name and you'll be taken to your home page, which is where we will do all of the set up.

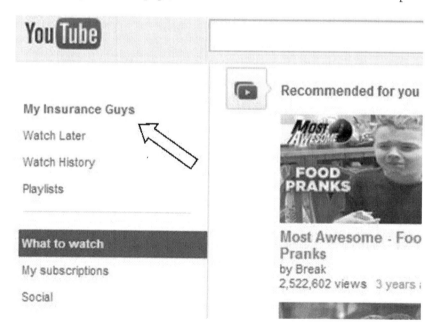

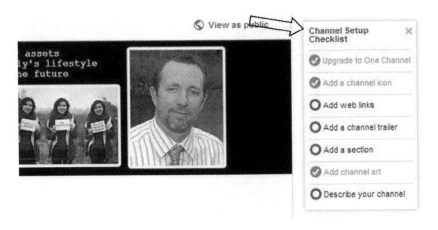

It's easy to work your way through the checklist, just click each item on the list. You will probably already have a "One Channel" YouTube page so the first thing on the list that you'll need to get done is add a channel icon. This is your profile picture and should be the same business picture of you that is also used with your other communication tools. You will also need to add your channel art, which is the display that shows above your videos, kind of like your Facebook cover photo. Because of YouTube's size requirements for the channel art, it is easier to have someone create it for you unless you are good at using Photoshop (I am not). For $5 you can get it made for you through Fiverr.com. Enter "YouTube Channel Art" into the search bar. At the time of this writing, there were 18,872 options to choose from.

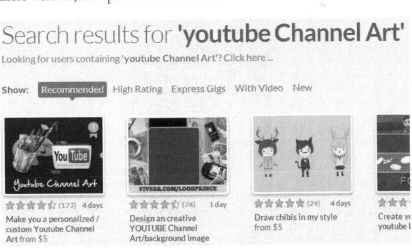

I actually hired two people so I could have a few designs to choose

129

from and then picked the design I liked the best. When describing what you want, reference your Facebook and Twitter accounts and let the designer know you want the channel art design to match. Here's the one I chose:

Paying $5 for someone else to do the work with the right dimensions that YouTube requires is well worth the money. If you like the design that you're given, you can usually pay another $5 for a matching Twitter background and $5 for a matching Facebook Cover photo. It's amazing how much $5 gets you these days! After you add your website and social media links to the "About" tab, they'll show up on your channel art as links so that people watching your videos can easily get to your other pages on the web.

Also on the list is making a channel trailer, the "Welcome" video that people will see when they visit your channel so they know what to expect from you and your videos. When you click on the "Create Trailer" button, you have the option of creating a video or uploading a video. If you don't have a video camera, phone with video capabilities or video editing software (all of which we'll talk about in the upcoming "Creating Videos Worth Watching" section), then click on create button and you can record your welcome video on the spot right through YouTube. We will go over everything you need to know to make good videos momentarily, but for now, it's just important to know that the trailer is something that needs to get done.

Creating sections will allow you to separate your videos into groups so new prospects and existing clients can easily find what they're looking for. You should have a section for auto insurance, home insurance, life insurance, new clients, existing clients...whatever else makes sense for your agency. Don't forget to completely fill out the channel description and everything else in the "About" tab. In about 10 minutes, you'll have a professional looking YouTube channel set up and ready for you to start adding videos.

Creating Videos Worth Watching

When you're ready to make your first video, click the upload button in the top tool bar next to the search icon. When you do, you'll have a few choices. You can select a file to upload from your computer if you already made a video with your phone or a video camera or you can record directly from YouTube using your computer's webcam. Either way will get things done, but there are a few things to consider first.

There are three T's that go into making videos worth watching, your Tech, your Talk and your Topics. First things first, let's talk Tech. You can create videos with your webcam, your cell phone or a real video camera. All 3 will get the job done, but there are some definite advantages to stopping by Best Buy and spending $100 on an actual video camera - preferably HD - and $50 on some basic editing software. Again, you CAN get by with your computer's webcam and you CAN do some basic editing through YouTube but if you're going to put yourself out there as the best agent in town, you might as well look as professional as possible (especially for new prospects). A real HD video camera will keep you from looking grainy on screen and give you better sound quality so the people watching your videos won't be turned off by the quality. I use a Bloggie and a very small tripod that sits on my desk to record my videos.

Basic editing software will allow you to trim your video of any unnecessary babbling and add in any graphics or annotations you would like your viewers to see. For example, I like to add my name and title at the beginning of each of my videos and my website at the end so anyone watching will know where to go to get more information. Most software packages available are designed with ease of use in mind and, after editing a few videos, you should be able to edit a 3-4 minute video in less than

10 minutes. You do not, however, have to buy editing software. YouTube has some built in editing capabilities that you can access by clicking the edit button next to any of your uploaded videos in your video manager.

After Tech, it's time to think about your Talk - what you're going to say. You should NOT script your entire video word for word as it will take away from your natural personality and come across as a planned speech. However, you should always, always, always outline your video so that you do not miss any important points or throw in any unimportant commentary. Your videos should be short and sweet, and the best way to stay on topic is to follow a bullet point outline of the important things you want to convey in your video.

Don't get hung up on your video being perfect because it never will be. There will always be mistakes, stutters and too many "umms" and "ahs", that is just the way it works. Your first few videos are going to seem to take forever and you're not going to be happy with them but I promise the more videos you make, the better they will become. The secret is to push through those first few videos so that you become proficient with the camera, the talking and the process that goes into making a 3-4 minute video. If you wait until you make a perfect video, you'll never make any video at all. If you eliminate every imperfection, it won't come across as real anyway.

After your Tech and your Talk, it's time to think about your Topics. What are you going to talk about that's going to be worth watching? The answer is a lot of things, more than you probably think. This is the time to go back to your editorial calendar and decide which part of each month's topic should be shared on camera. Which part of the topic is more emotional? Which piece is a little more difficult to explain or harder to understand? Those are the parts that you can convey through an actual conversation in a way that is easy for your clients and prospects to follow along with.

For your current clients, try to come up with one or two videos per month, max. One is enough to accomplish your goals and reach out to the clients who prefer to watch rather than listen or read. More than two and you're going to start to overwhelm your clients with more information than they can handle. The goal is to provide constant reminders of who you are, what you do and how you can help without coming across as pushy, salesy or overbearing. One fun, informative or educational video each month will do the trick. You'll probably find that most clients don't watch the monthly videos but that's okay because the reminder is still there. Those that do watch will be watching for a reason. They'll have something going on in their life that your video can relate to or help with and, if you do a good job in your video, they will come to you for follow up information, advice and help with their situation. This is where the magic happens; when clients call you and ask you to help solve their problem!

You don't need to make ongoing videos for your prospects, but rather, a video library to answer the questions that new prospects and potential clients commonly ask. What liability limits should I choose? What affects my car insurance premiums? What discounts are available? Why should I do business with you? Make a list of every question you get from new prospects and make a quick video (2-4 minutes long) that can be accessed in your library or emailed out as a part of your new prospect follow up campaign. According to a study conducted by the Sales & Marketing Executives Club of Los Angeles, 81% of sales are made after the 4th contact, but 90% of agents stop trying after 3 contacts (7). Having some "go to", informative touches lined up for your prospects will bring in more business because you will be touching your prospects over and over again until they are ready to buy.

A video library works great for new clients as well, to show them more about your agency, the various products you sell and the different ways you can help their family.

Here are a few more important things to keep in mind when making or uploading videos to YouTube: First of all, make sure you choose "public" for your videos privacy setting if you want the world to see it or "unlisted" if you want people to have to use a link to find it (it won't show up in YouTube searches). Give your videos as many relevant tags as you can think of (always add your name as a tag too so it starts to show up in Google and YouTube searches) and a basic description so that search engines, and the people using them, have a sense of what your video is going to be about. You have to choose a category for each video that you make and most videos will fall into either the "People & Blogs" or the "Autos & Vehicles" category.

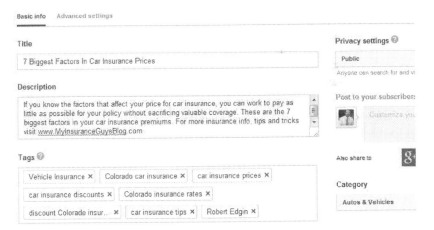

After The Videos Are Made

Just like every other tool we've discussed, you have to take action for others to see it and appreciate it. You have to share it, link it to your other tools and let your clients and prospects know about it. You can share videos directly through your YouTube account by going into a video and choosing the "share" button. You'll have options to share with a link or directly through any of your social media accounts. You can also embed a video directly into your blog or email it right from YouTube, although I prefer to email from my own email account using the link so that my email signature and any other information I want to share will be in the email.

Now is the time to create playlists and add your video to one (or more) playlists so that your videos are organized for your clients and prospects to be able to easily find what they're looking for.

You should look for as many ways to share your videos as possible. You can add a link to your welcome video in the signature of your email. You should link to a video in your blog posts if they share a topic or if the video is the next part of the topic in your editorial calendar. You can list a direct link in your newsletter or a mailing, tweet about it and more.

There are so many ways to integrate video into your agency that you'll never get around to using all of them. As a 21st Century Communication tool, the options are endless. Start small and try to post a video or two per month to get the ball rolling. Then, sit down and think about your agency's overall communication plan and how you want video to fit in. It can be a lead generator, a client insulator, an education tool, a method for cross-selling, part of a follow up system…or all of the above. Just take it slow and don't get overwhelmed or freaked out the first time you watch yourself on video. Just like all of the other tools we've talked about, the more you do it, the better it will be.

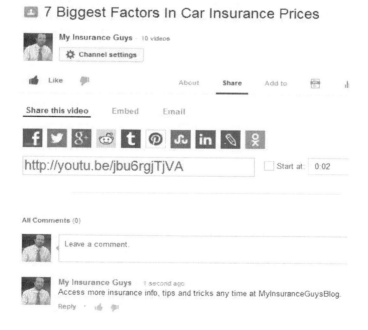

VIDEOMAIL - THE NEW EMAIL

It's no surprise that we're talking about email as a tool in your 21ˢᵗ Century Communication toolbox. Email has become one of the most preferred methods of communicating in the world. Email is trackable, there are no limits on the length of the message, messages can be delivered to multiple people at the same time…email makes our lives easier. However, for professionals who want to use email as a way to communicate with clients, there are some challenges that have to be dealt with if you want your communication to be effective (or even seen).

The average person receives 75 emails per day, according to a study done by the Radacati Group (Radacati.com) and spends between 60 and 150 minutes each day dealing with emails. That's 81 days per year checking, deleting, writing, sending and dealing with emails. Many workers now complain about "email overload" and cite it as one of the main reasons they cannot keep up with their required office duties. Email is also the most abused form of communication, evidenced by the hundreds of emails in your spam folder every week. It is far too common to be contacted daily by salesman, crooks, kings in Nigeria with millions they need help moving out of the country, foreign lotteries that somehow drew your name and long lost relatives who need your social security number in order to get you your share of an inheritance. People are not only overwhelmed by the **amount** of emails they receive each day, they are also suspicious of the emails they receive throughout the day that are not from someone in their inner circle.

While email represents one of the biggest opportunities for communicating with your clients and prospects, it represents some of the biggest challenges as well: **getting noticed, getting read** (or heard) and **getting a response**. If your email is one of the 75 that your client receives on any given day and it looks just like the other 74 emails they've received, why would anyone take the time to read yours? Your emails need to stand out, be different and immediately get your clients and prospects interested enough to click into your message and see what you have to say. Sending video mail (VM) instead of email will help make

137

sure that happens.

Video mail has a much better chance of getting noticed because there is an immediate and unmistakable difference in the way a VM looks compared to a normal, boring email. The first thing my clients and prospects see is my smiling face looking at them. Not opening the email would almost be the equivalent of looking me in the eye and telling me to go away and most people would never do that. They also know (or at least think) that I've made a personal video just for them so it must be something pretty important and, let's be honest, VM is still the exception to what everyone else is sending and most people will click into the message just for the coolness factor.

Once a client or prospect sees your VM and clicks into the message, you have a much better chance of your message being heard and understood than if you were typing out a long message that your client will have to sit and take the time to read. If a picture is worth a thousand words, how much is a video worth? Email vs. video mail is the equivalent of trying to do all of your client meetings and sales calls through a letter instead of face to face. Which way will get a better result?

When you send a video mail, you can convey emotion and a sense of urgency. You can avoid misunderstandings that might come from trying to read what you mean and you can let people get to know you better and connect with you and your personality. Video mail is your opportunity to look people in the eye and say "this is what you need to do and this is why you need to do it with me." Clients and prospects not only watch the VM that I send them and get the message I want them to hear, often times they watch it repeatedly AND share it with their friends and family!

Most VM providers will show you how many times a video has been viewed and it is not uncommon for someone to watch a video 5 or 6 times. There have been numerous occasions where a client has emailed me a question about coverage and I've responded with a video mail to explain the answer and then a day or two later I receive a phone call from my client's neighbor or coworker who wants to discuss their coverage because they saw one of my VM's. I often get referred by prospects before I even meet with them to review their policies because they want their friends to see the cool way their insurance guy communicated with them. If you want your message to be heard and understood, send it in a VM. Here's a message that was viewed by a prospect 9 times!

Inbox (17)
Bulk Mail
Drafts
Templates
Send Later
Sent Items
Trash   Journal (228)
Docusign
Fire Brush   (6)
Monthly contest entry
Newsletter Request

Sender	Subject	Date	Size
Chris Anderson	Fwd: Pics	9:11 am	2.4 m
Moody Insurance Group	How to Sell Health Insurance in a Small Business World	7:16 am	11 k
Eject Notification	[Eject Alert] pastorsj@gmail.com has viewed your message	Mon, 9:54 pm	8 k
Eject Notification	[Eject Alert] pastorsj@gmail.com has viewed your message	Mon, 9:04 pm	8 k
Eject Notification	[Eject Alert] pastorsj@gmail.com has viewed your message	Mon, 8:54 pm	8 k
Eject Notification	[Eject Alert] pastorsj@gmail.com has viewed your message	Mon, 8:44 pm	8 k
Eject Notification	[Eject Alert] pastorsj@gmail.com has viewed your message	Mon, 8:24 pm	8 k
Eject Notification	[Eject Alert] pastorsj@gmail.com has viewed your message	Mon, 7:54 pm	6 k
Eject Notification	[Eject Alert] pastorsj@gmail.com has viewed your message	Mon, 6:24 pm	8 k
Eject Notification	[Eject Alert] pastorsj@gmail.com has viewed your message	Mon, 5:14 pm	8 k
r.edgin@weinsurecolorado...	Free Rport Or Newsletter Request	Mon, 4:54 pm	2 k
Eject Notification	[Eject Alert] pastorsj@gmail.com has viewed your message	Mon, 4:44 pm	8 k
Johnna Foster-Miller	RE: Follow Up From Friday Phone Call	Mon, 12:11 pm	95 k

Video mail also has a much better response rate than normal emails because you can actually tell people, with your own voice, what it is you want or need them to do. You can ask them a question or make a request and explain why it's important. You can even beg and plead with someone if you need to. Ignoring your VM would be just like someone ignoring you. Most people aren't going to do it.

What Should You Use Video mail for?

You probably send a number of emails to your clients and prospects every single day to answer questions, send ID cards, remind people of appointments and invite them in to your office for an annual review. If you're one of the relatively few agents who has an actual marketing plan, you may even try to solicit business or cross-sell through email campaigns. All of those activities can be done more efficiently and effectively using video mail. Not only will your VM get noticed, get read (seen and heard) and get a response, it will also be easier on you. I type at an average speed of 45 words per minute, so if I have to answer someone's question or explain a piece of coverage that takes 450 words to explain, I'll spend 10 minutes composing an email. However, the average person speaks at about 150 words per minute, so if I send a VM instead of an email, I'll cut my work time by 2/3 AND be able to give a better explanation than if I were typing.

In addition to all of the typical emails that you send each day, VM can be used to deliver messages that you probably are NOT currently sending out through regular email. Video mail can be used to send out a personal introduction to new prospects before you call them back with their proposals or ask them to come into the office. It can be used to deliver proposals to people who prefer to work through email (a growing number of people). If you're forced to do business online, at least a VM will allow your prospect to connect with who you are and get to know you a little. A personal "thank you" goes a long way when expressed through VM, as do your well-wishes, thoughts and prayers that you send out to clients who are going through a tough time. Congratulatory VM's are always appreciated and they are a great way to send out a simple "thinking of you" message with a special report that your client or prospect may be interested in.

Another great use of VM in my office is our birthday message. Every year I record a new message and then my staff sends it out to each client on the morning of their birthday. It's less time consuming than calling each client and it's a more personal message than a call from my office staff. Clients seem to love it and will often watch their birthday video 3 or 4 times.

When you receive the birthday VM, you can immediately tell it's going to be a fun message. There are balloons and a birthday hat and even a special picture that can be opened (see next page).

One of the best VM's in terms of return on my time and investment is my monthly "video minute" that is emailed out to each of my clients and prospects once per month. Each month, I pick two topics (one insurance and one financial) to briefly discuss through a VM in order to educate my clients and provide some extra value from my office. Not surprisingly, my monthly topics are tied to my topic of the month and include links to my blog and an offer for more information through a special report, book, white paper, etc. I give my clients something to raise their hand for in order to find out if any of them want or need to be sold what I have to offer. Every month I get a flood of responses from my video minute about not only, the special offer I'm making, but about a whole list of other things clients have been meaning to call me about. I receive questions and requests for things they need, I receive a bunch of "thank yous" for providing the information and sometimes I even get referrals.

The video minute reminds my client that my office is there and working hard to make sure they are taken care of. Even if they don't need anything and don't respond, they at least see my face, hear my name and are reminded of all of the things we can do for them. I always start my video minute with the same opening sentence; "Hi, this is Robert

Edgin, your favorite insurance and financial advisor, with the video minute for (month and year)." My clients hear that I am their favorite insurance and financial guy 12 times per year!

One of the great things about video mail is the ability to create a generic message that seems as if you're talking specifically to one person and then use it as a template anytime the same situation comes up. The birthday message is one example, but there are plenty of other opportunities to send pre-built VM's to clients and prospects. We use them for directions to our office, reminders about annual reviews, introductions to our office and more.

Video mail doesn't have to be expensive either. There are a number of services out there that charge a low monthly fee or an annual plan for sending your VM's. You can even find a few free services but I would not recommend using them because they contain ads and they don't allow you to control the look of the video mail. Make sure you choose a service that allows you to brand your page with your personal information. You'll notice that my VM contains a list of links to all of my other websites and social media, as well as, my contact information. Clients can also respond directly through the email by hitting "reply" (not always possible through the free services) and even look at my video business card if they want to. I can also attach multiple items to my VM for my client's review, which is very important.

143

I use a company called Eyejot for my office VM because it is simple, easy for my clients and prospects, completely customizable and very inexpensive. For only $100 per year, I can reach my clients and prospects in a unique and personal way. They have 3 choices of plans ranging from free to ProPlus (my plan) to fit your needs. However, I strongly urge you to get one of the two pay plans to remove the ads. If you have staff, this is a great tool for them to use as well and extremely cost effective. It's important for your staff to be known as a part of the office the same way you are. The more your clients and prospects see your staff's face, the more trust they will have in them and their ability to handle things when you are unavailable.

You can see the three plan options for Eyejot on the next page and I've included a special web address to get signed up for your own plan.

Account Comparison	free	pro	pro+
Maximum Recording Duration	5 minutes	10 minutes	15 minutes
Inbox Expiration	1 month	never	never
Unlimited Messages	✔	✔	✔
Send to any Email Address	✔	✔	✔
Visual Address Book	✔	✔	✔
Address Book Import	✔	✔	✔
Site Widget	✔	✔	✔
iTunes/RSS Support	✔	✔	✔
Video Uploading		✔	✔
Enhanced Mobile Inbox		✔	✔
Advertising Free		✔	✔
Add your own logo and color scheme to Eyejot's notification elements			✔
Receive alerts when your video messages have been viewed			✔
Attach documents to your video messages			✔
Price	FREE	$29.95 / year	$99.95 / year

Out of all of the tools we discussed so far, video mail is the easiest to implement and use. It gives you an excellent return on your investment of time and money and it will definitely elevate you in the minds of your clients and prospects. You're going to email people every day. You might as well do it in a way that is memorable and sets you apart from the rest of the agents in town. Here is the link to sign up for your own Eyejot account: **http://goo.gl/4KdDl4**

NEWSLETTERS

I love, love, love newsletters! Actually, let me be more specific. I love, love, love the power that a newsletter brings, the professional status it conveys, the sales it produces and the consistent results it delivers. Nothing in the 21st Century Communication toolbox creates more talk and more action from my clients. No other tool is anticipated and read like my newsletter and no other tool allows me to get as good of a return on my time and money as my newsletter. In other words, a well written newsletter is the bomb! It's all that AND a bag of chips! It's the answer to world hunger and a way to get democrats and republicans to see eye to eye! Okay, those last two are a bit of a stretch, but just barely.

When done properly, a newsletter will do more for your agency's success than any other tool at your disposal. It gives you the opportunity to let people into your personal life in meaningful ways, share tips and information that solidifies you as an insurance professional, ask for referrals, remind people of everything you do, cross-sell and increase retention all at the same time in one mailing. There is no better way to accomplish so much or reach so many and nothing will be more read or produce a better response than your monthly newsletter.

I spend 5 - 10 hours per month creating my monthly newsletter. It takes quite a bit of time to fill 6 pages with articles, tips and tricks that will be well received and appreciated by clients, but every hour produces multiples of what it costs me in cross-sales, referrals and retention. I promise, it is well worth the effort! Don't worry, I'm going to share my secrets to make your newsletter as painless and easy for you as possible but you will be required to work and put in some time for this particular tool.

Because of the time, effort and energy involved with making a personal newsletter each month, a lot of agents rely on pre-packaged and "done for you" newsletters. With one exception (at the end of this chapter), I would **strongly encourage you to create your own personal newsletter** and NOT use the template, "done for you" newsletters available for purchase. Why? Because they don't produce results! If all you're looking for is something to give your clients with your name and picture on it that they can quickly and easily throw away, a "done for you" newsletter will work just fine. If you want people to actually read your newsletter, talk to you about the different articles and call you to set appointments based on your newsletter material, you need to do the work to create your own.

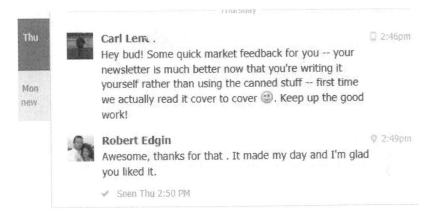

If all of your other communication comes across as a personal connection to you and your office, your newsletter needs to do the same. Pre-packaged newsletters have a corporate look and feel so there is a disconnect between your newsletter and all of your other communication tools when your clients or prospects read them. When I meet with clients for their annual review, it is not uncommon for them to ask me about things I've written about in the newsletter. Sometimes I get calls or emails following up on a personal event or situation I discussed just to make sure things are okay.

Last year, my father had a heart attack that really put a scare into my entire family. He survived and made a full recovery. I shared some of what I learned from the ordeal in my next newsletter in order to pass along some information I thought my clients should know. The response to that newsletter was amazing! I couldn't believe the number of clients who called in or emailed me to check on my dad. I received tips on how to recover from other clients who had been through similar situations. I was sent articles on heart healthy diets and exercise routines so I could pass them along to my dad and for months, almost every client that came into the office inquired about my dad's recovery.

99% of my clients had never met my father but they knew about him because they had been following along with my family adventures for years. The response I received from that edition of my newsletter was a great reminder that people want more than an insurance professional, they want someone they can feel connected to. Business is so cold and corporate, especially our business where more people than ever are working with call centers and on line chat boxes. If you can create a business environment that also connects with people in a personal way, you'll have some of the best retention in the industry.

If I haven't sold you on the value of a newsletter by now, I probably never will. So, let's get down to business and start building your own personal newsletter. The initial set up will take you a few hours but it will be well worth the effort.

Before we go through the setup of your newsletter, I thought it might be helpful to see a sample issue.

MARCH | 2013

Insurance & Money Matters

Robert Edgin
Academy National Ins.
5155 W. Academy Blvd, Ste. 100
Colo. Spgs., CO 80918
719.685.8585

OUR MISSION IS SIMPLE: WE PROTECT OUR CLIENT'S ASSETS, PRESERVE OUR CLIENT'S LIFESTYLE AND PREPARE OUR CLIENTS FOR RETIREMENT.

2012 was another great year here at the office and I was fortunate to be named the Agent of the Year for our 8 state region. However, during the first month of 2013 I found myself helping two different families file death claims for loved ones who passed away far too young - one was under 40 and the other under 30.

Helping families make financial decisions after the loss of a breadwinner, spouse, mother, father, husband or wife is a necessary part of my job, and even though I know the life insurance that both families had in place will go a long way to preserve their lifestyles, these types of months remind me that there are a lot of things more important in life than being the Agent of the Year. Helping families, and taking care of my own, is far more rewarding than any awards you can win.

Speaking of my family, we had a recent conversation about what my kids call the "Edgin Curse" after I spent a night in the Hospital while on a family vacation in Cozumel (see page 3). They're convinced that we have more crazy, unusual and bad things happen to our family than any other family they know. I'm not one to believe in curses, but I do believe in odds. I told Taylor and Christian that you can eliminate 90% of the things that go wrong simply by eliminating 90% of the fun things we do. I've always made it a point to expose my family to as many adventures as possible - travel, scuba, camping, etc. - and the more adventures you have, the more opportunities there are for things to go wrong. If I would have been home, sitting on the couch watching TV instead of chasing a turtle 80 feet under water, I would NOT have spent the night in the hospital. But where's the fun in that? How many memories can you make sitting on the couch watching TV?

It's all about exposure and your willingness to open yourself up to the adventures and the consequences, both good and bad, that come with those adventures. If you're not comfortable or willing to deal with the possible hiccups that come with certain activities, don't expose yourself to those activities. Every person and family has a different tolerance level for what they can and are willing to deal with. I feel like we have some great adventures, but compared to a lot of you out there, I feel pretty tame! I have clients who spend 10 days in the woods by themselves living off the land. There are race car drivers, sky divers and a few Olympic hopefuls out there doing things that I'm both jealous and a little scared of!

Kylah gets a little worried every once in a while about some of the places we go and the things we do, and honestly, I'm glad I have her to keep some of my adventures from ever leaving the idea stage (she's a great balance for me). My goal is to go and see and do as many things as I possibly can for as long as I possibly can and, fortunately, at the end of the conversation with my kids, neither of them were willing to eliminate the "Edgin Curse" by eliminating our family adventures.

I hope 2013 is a year filled with adventures and exposure to new things for my family and yours. Dealing with a "family curse" is a lot better than dealing with the boredom of never going anywhere or doing anything. Most of the little mishaps aren't really that big of a deal as long as you don't put yourself in a position where you could really get hurt, or worse. You create a lot more memories through the crazy stuff than you ever will sitting on the couch watching TV. Besides, the stories are a lot better and you get a lot more pictures when you're out there creating family adventures!

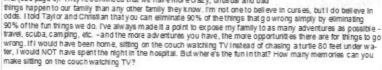

Page one is always my personal thoughts on current events or a specific situation or time of year. It allows my clients and prospects to hear my personality and voice on a given subject.

2013 REFERRAL REWARDS PROGRAM!

This year we are using the Referral Rewards Program to celebrate a unique, unusual or unknown holiday each month. There are so many great holidays out there that you've never heard of, and we can't wait to share them with you!

In honor of National Potato Chip Day, we're giving away some gourmet chips as a way of saying "thanks" for your introductions!

Introduce a friend, coworker or family member to our office during the month of March and receive a Gourmet Potato Chip Gift Basket! Have them call today for an insurance proposal and grab yourself some seriously delicious chips!

POTATO CHIP GIFT BASKETS WILL BE HAND DELIVERED AT THE END OF THE MONTH!

A big "thank you" goes out to all of our great clients who introduced us to someone last month and got a gourmet popcorn gift box as a token of our appreciation. Thank you:

Tom & Charlene Jennings

Garland & Di Foust

Jay & Sharon Quinng

MJ Coon

Gary & Amy Martinez

Kent & Megan Sours

Office Classifieds

Although we see a lot of cool cars and other toys that our clients are picking up or restoring, we don't have too many opportunities to try and help our clients sell their rides. Especially not rides as nice as this 1969 Ford Mustang, and certainly not at such a great price - $11,000! If you, or someone you know, is interested in a great classic car, give me a call at the office and I'll introduce you to the seller.

Does anyone need some part time help now through the first week of August? My 17 year old, Taylor, is looking to branch out and do some work (for someone other than me) before she moves to California in August. She's great with people and loves to be on the move, so a waitress position or anything that requires a lot of get up and go would be perfect for her. She does need a little flexibility with her evening dance schedule but she will work hard for you. She is trying to save up as much money as she can for her big move. If you know of anyone looking for a bright young worker, please give me a call at the office so we can chat!

Happy National Potato Chip Day!

March 14th is National Potato Chip Day! In celebration of the mighty chip, you're encouraged to eat potato chips at every meal on this special day. Here are a few fun facts you may not know about the chip:

1. Potato chips were invented in 1853 by a chef in Saratoga Springs, NY, by a chef who's picky customer kept sending his French fries back because they were too thick.
2. Potato chips are the #1 snack food in America, with 1.2 billion pounds eaten each year.
3. It takes 1000 pounds of potato's to make 350 pounds of potato chips.
4. Some popular potato chip flavors around the world include: ketchup, roast chicken, paprika, Kebab (Egypt), mint (India), mayonnaise (Japan), and pizza (Serbia).
5. The average person eats 6 pounds of potato chips every year.

"Thank you for continuing to develop your skills and abilities to better suit your clients needs and busy schedules. You truly are a pleasure to work with in a field where pleasantries are not always found."

Shelley Savage

I always dedicate a section of my newsletter to my "Referral Rewards" program. This is where I thank people for their referrals from the last month and remind everyone that not only do we love referrals, we reward them as well!

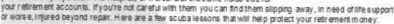

What A Scuba Diving Accident And Night In A Mexican Hospital Reminded Me About Investing

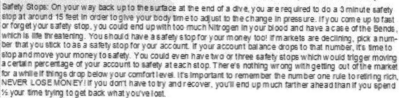

I recently spent the night in a Mexican hospital while on a family vacation in Cozumel. A scuba diving accident gave me a case of Vertigo that needed immediate medical attention. Although I had to end my week of diving after only one day, I made a full recovery and, luckily, all is well that ends well. I was "forced" to spend 6 days sitting on the beach under a palm tree watching the waves roll in. There are worse ways to recover!

My accident and overnight stay reminded me of a few scuba diving lessons that also apply to investing for retirement. If you're not careful when you're diving, you can end up injured, in the hospital, or worse. But the same holds true for your retirement accounts. If you're not careful with them you can find them slipping away, in need of life support or worse, injured beyond repair. Here are a few scuba lessons that will help protect your retirement money:

Safety Stops: On your way back up to the surface at the end of a dive, you are required to do a 3 minute safety stop at around 15 feet in order to give your body time to adjust to the change in pressure. If you come up too fast or forget your safety stop, you could end up with too much Nitrogen in your blood and have a case of the Bends, which is life threatening. You should have a safety stop for your money too! If markets are declining, pick a number that you stick to as a safety stop for your account. If your account balance drops to that number, it's time to stop and move your money to safety. You could even have two or three safety stops which would trigger moving a certain percentage of your account to safety at each stop. There's nothing wrong with getting out of the market for a while if things drop below your comfort level. It's important to remember the number one rule to retiring rich, NEVER LOSE MONEY! If you don't have to try and recover, you'll end up much farther ahead than if you spend ½ your time trying to get back what you've lost.

Pressurize often: My injury was caused from a "reverse block", too much pressure in my ear that wasn't released by pressurizing on my way up. The result could be a blown ear drum (mine was very close to being blown) which causes dizziness, loss of balance and nausea. You should pressurize your retirement account when it is headed up by keeping your account balanced and not letting it get over weighted in any one type of investment. If you find one of your holdings growing faster than the rest, periodically rebalance your account so you have the right portfolio diversification that both protects your account from losing and still allows it to grow. It can be tempting to leave too much of your money in an over performing investment. If markets turn in a hurry, the fastest growing investment often becomes the fastest losing investment and you end up with less money than you started with and have to play catch up again. Two steps forward and three steps back is a bad strategy for your retirement money!

Know when to ask for help: My original plan was to rest for a day and then go back to diving. If I would have, I would probably never be able to dive again. My Vertigo got so bad that I was unable to sit, stand or walk. I should have gone to the hospital well before I reached that point but my stubborn thinking that "I would be all right" kept me suffering for far longer than I needed to. It wasn't until I was diagnosed and treated that I started to recover and feel better. There's no reason to try and hang on by yourself with your retirement account either. There are so many professionals who know how to diagnose problems and prescribe the right strategy to keep your investments healthy and growing for your future. If you start to feel overwhelmed about the choices for your investments or unsure of what you need to do to protect your account, set up a review with a professional that you know and trust and give your retirement account the best chance possible to be big and healthy when it's time to start using it. The longer you put off getting the help you need, the harder it is to make a full recovery!

I lost a week of scuba diving, but fortunately I'll be back in the water and diving again on my next trip. Things could have been much worse for me if I wouldn't have received the medical help I needed. If you haven't given your retirement accounts a checkup in a while, or feel like they're not as healthy as they should be, call the office and set up a quick review. We can diagnose any problems and make sure you have a prescription for the best retirement possible.

I try to turn my personal stories and life events into learning experiences for my clients and prospects. People will read stories much more often and in depth than a straight learning or "how to" article.

Do You Need Gap Insurance?

If you're ever going to buy a new car again and finance the purchase, you've got a GAP that you need to think about as you're pulling out of the lot. Everyone knows what happens when you buy a new car; by the time you get it home it's already worth less than what you paid for it. After a about 18 months it's lost about 30% of its value, but how much do you still owe? If you owe more than your new car is worth, that's your GAP. If you crash that car you could be faced with a large sum of money to cover the GAP that your insurance policy does not pay for.

How GAP Insurance works: As the name implies, it insures against any GAP you may have between what your car is worth and what you owe. So, for example, let's say you go buy that new car you've had your eye on. The purchase price of the new car is $25,000 and you put $2,500 down. You finance $22,500 and start making your monthly payments. 18 month's later, you crash the car and it is totally destroyed. Your car insurance company is going to pay you what the car is worth, probably around $17,500. Unfortunately, you still owe $20,000 which means there is a $2,500 GAP that is still owed to pay off the destroyed car. If you have GAP insurance, the $2,500 will be paid for you. If you don't, you owe that money yourself.

There are two places you can buy GAP insurance, through the dealership that sells you your new car, or though your insurance agent. BUT, one of the two will cost you 300% more!

Through the dealership: One of the biggest up sales at the dealership is GAP insurance. They charge a fortune for it (usually around $400) and then add it into your financing. Financing $400 over 5 years at 5.5% ends up costing you $470. That's not bad compared to paying the extra $7000 that Joe got stuck with, BUT it's a heck of a lot more than you need to pay. Instead of getting your GAP insurance through the dealership, get it from your local, professional insurance agent for a fraction of the cost.

Through your insurance company: GAP insurance can be added directly to your car insurance policy for around $12 per 6 months. It's the same coverage and the same protection, but the total cost over 5 years is $120. That's a savings of $350 just because of where you bought your GAP insurance. Make sure your insurance company knows if you are buying or leasing, as that can have an effect on the GAP protection.

Any time you can save $350 AND get the same protection, you've made a wise financial decision. Make sure you buy GAP insurance if you need it, but DON'T buy it from the dealerships or you'll be paying too much!

Recipe Of The Month - Chocolate Covered Potato Chip

Ridged potato chips are dipped into tempered milk chocolate for an elegant treat that everyone will enjoy.

Ingredients: 1 pound of high quality milk   8 cups ridged potato chips
              chocolate, chopped

Step 1: Place about 3/4 of the chocolate into a heat safe bowl, and place over the top of a pan of simmering water. If you have a double boiler, use that. Heat, stirring occasionally until the chocolate has melted, then continue to heat the chocolate to 110 degrees F (43 degrees C), stirring occasionally. You may use a meat thermometer if your candy thermometer does not go that low.

Step 2: As soon as the melted chocolate reaches temperature, remove it from the heat, and stir in the remaining chopped chocolate until melted. Continue stirring until the chocolate has cooled to 90 degrees F (32 degrees C). Touching a dab of chocolate to your lip will feel cool.

Step 3: Use tongs to dip potato chips one at a time into the chocolate. Place on waxed paper starting at the point farthest from you and working your way in so as not to drip on your finished chips. Cool until set. You may refrigerate if you like.

I look for multiple ways to get people involved with my newsletter and appeal to as many different types of people as possible. That is why I always include a recipe of the month. I always tie the recipe in to my referral reward or theme of the month.

Exercise Your Brain For A Chance To Win Dinner!

Studies have long since proven that exercising your brain gives you more creativity and helps you live a longer, more satisfying life AND a new study by Robert Edgin shows it can also earn you $30 for dinner at The Olive Garden! Okay, it's not an official study, but if you get the brain teasers correct, I'll enter you into my monthly drawing for a $2 gift certificate for each correct answer! The deadline to enter is 4/15/13

In honor of the potato chip, this month's "exercise your brain" is all about the chip. Answer these trivia questions for your chance to win. Each correct answer is worth one entry!

1. How much money is spent on potato chips every year in the United States?

2. What are the 2 most popular potato chip flavors in the United States?

3. What were potato chips originally called?

4. What year was the first potato chip factory built?

Email your entries to: r.edgin@weinsurecolorado.com or Fax your entries to: 719-630-1101
mail them in or drop them by the office

> Congratulations to last month's brain challenge winner: Sandy and Dustin Rupe! Sandy and Dustin won $25 to spend at Jamba Juice and Baskin Robbins.

Tax Season Is Almost Here!

You're probably getting ready to file your taxes and, hopefully, get some money back. But if you're not taking advantage of all of the IRS deductions that you're allowed, you're leaving money on the table. One of the simplest and best IRS deductions is the fully deductible IRA. Not only do you get a dollar for dollar deduction against your earnings, you get to keep the money you put into an IRA and spend it on yourself in the future!

Most IRA deductions are for money spent on expenses, but the IRA deduction is a tax savings on money you keep for yourself, making it the smartest tax deduction in existence today. Here's an example of how it works:

1. Let's say you have paid taxes all year, but you just found out from your CPA that you still owe $1000. You are in the 25% tax bracket - you pay 25% of your income in taxes.
2. You move $4,000 from your savings account into a tax-deductible IRA. The $4,000 acts as a direct reducer of your income.
3. You no longer have to pay the 25% tax on $4,000 of income due to the deduction, which saves you $1,000 in taxes and eliminates your tax bill. The $4,000 is still your money, but now it will grow tax-deferred until you are ready to spend it in the future when you retire.

Of course, there are some simple rules that have to be followed as far as income limits and contributions go, but if you're facing a tax bill and you have NOT contributed to your IRA, call me to get together for an IRA review so we can make sure you pay as little tax as possible and keep more of your money to spend in retirement!

Tired Of Telemarketers?

If you're tired of getting those telemarketing calls, you can add your phone number to the national Do Not Call Registry in under two minutes. You can add your cell phone too! Clarissa, a great client of mine, alerted me to the fact cell phone numbers went public in January. This means that telemarketers can start calling your cell phone instead of your home phone to try and reach you. To limit those unwanted calls, all you need to do is call 888-382-1222 and enter the number you want added. It will add your number to the registry for 5 years and remove your number from telemarketing lists. Thanks Clarissa!

Contests are another way to get people involved. My monthly "Exercise Your Brain" section always brings in a lot of responses from my clients.

Robert Edgin
American National Ins.
5155 N Academy Blvd, Ste. 100
Colo. Spgs., CO 80918
719.685.8585

"Thank you Robert! We appreciate you and your wonderful office staff! You're a great team!!"
God Bless, Ruth Miller

We've Gone Virtual For Those That Need It!

We all lead busier lives with more hectic schedules than ever before, but reviewing your insurance is still important!

I love the opportunities I have to sit down face to face with my clients. We catch up and visit, we look for missing discounts or excess coverage, and we make sure that if something goes wrong that we have the right coverage in place to be protected. Insurance rules change from year to year, as do your insurance needs if you have things going on in your life. It's important to get together every 12 - 24 months for a quick refresher of all of the things that are (and are not) covered by your insurance.

In order to make that easier for our busy clients, we launched a virtual review program last year to test it out and see if it worked. The results have been fantastic! I can meet with clients through the computer and still allow you to see me talking to you AND see what's on my computer so I can actually SHOW you your policy and changes that might be affecting you. It's simple, easy, and requires no technical know how. Here's what Shelly had to say about it:

"I wanted to follow up with you regarding our Go-To-Meeting exchange on August 25th. I found the experience to be very user friendly and very convenient. It allowed me to see the documents, and have a face to face conversation with you, without the hassle of driving to your office. I would definitely use this form of communication in the future."

If you're having a hard time making it to the office for a review, let's get virtual!

I send my newsletter as a 3 page (front and back for 6 total pages) fold over that gets double tabbed and labeled at my mail house. I always remind people to join me online for even more tips, tricks and giveaways.

Setting Up Your Newsletter

It's a good idea to be consistent with your newsletter, consistent with

153

the look, the feel and the timing. You want your clients and prospects to get used to your personal newsletter so they know what to expect and have something to look forward to each time they receive it. The first step is to choose a look for your newsletter that you like and can stick with for years to come.

Don't worry, there's no reason to start from scratch when it comes time to build your newsletter. There are plenty of free and templates for purchase available online to choose from and if you go to Google and type in "newsletter template", you'll get thousands of options. You can use a number of different programs for the actual construction of your newsletter but I would recommend Publisher because of the flexibility and ease of use it gives you. If you visit Microsoft's website, you can choose from a number of Publisher templates that are ready for download. Don't experiment with different templates each month as it will just confuse your clients. Whichever template you end up with, make sure you stick with it. **If you don't think you have the computer know how to build your newsletter using Publisher, there is some help available at the end of this chapter.**

There is no right or wrong when it comes to choosing your newsletter template but there are a few things to keep in mind. First, your newsletter should be physically mailed to your best clients and prospects, which means you are going to have to pay for printing. You should always print your newsletter for your best clients (A and B clients) and prospects in color. If you have a lot of lower level clients (C and D type clients), it may be okay to send them a black and white newsletter or a digital copy but your best clients get your best stuff - including a hard copy, color newsletter. When choosing a template, pick one that has a good ratio of color AND white area. You can see in my example that I use color for my headlines as well as some color accents on each page but I don't get too overwhelming with my colors.

You'll also see from my newsletter example that I use a lot of pictures. Every article or section of your newsletter should include a relevant picture for a number of reasons. For starters, most people are very visual. The first thing they do is look at the pictures on each page of your newsletter to see if it looks interesting to them. If the pictures don't capture their attention, they may not even read the headline of the corresponding article or section. It's a great idea to include yourself in at least one or two of the pictures each month so your clients and prospects can see your face. Pictures also help fill space so that it is a little bit easier to fill up a multi-page newsletter.

The feel of your newsletter also needs to be consistent each month. You shouldn't go from 6 pages one month to 3 the next. Pick a number of pages and keep it the same every month. If you need to hold something back because you have to much content for one month, that's a better idea than changing the feel of your newsletter and throwing off your clients by adding in extra pages. The tone of your newsletter also needs to match up with your other types of communication so that people still feel your perspective and your voice coming through in the newsletter.

After people start reading your different blog posts, facebook statuses and other articles, they'll get a sense of your voice - the way you write or communicate that portrays who you are. Don't change that when you're putting together your newsletter. If you are normally fun and easy going, maintain that in your newsletter. If you become straight business or cold in your newsletter while you are the opposite in all of your other communication, your clients and prospects will think that you are not being genuine or sincere. Alternately, if you are business-like in all of your day to day communication with your clients, don't try to become the life of the party in your newsletter. You are who you are, own it, be proud of it and stick to it in all of your communication tools.

The 50/50 rule applies to your newsletter just as it does for all of your other communication. If your newsletter is nothing but insurance education, you're not going to get many people to read it. At least 50% of your newsletter should be non-insurance information. It should be personal, social, fun and helpful - anything but "Insurance 101". If you must have more than 50% insurance information in one month's issue, at least try to make it fun or entertaining. For example, teach a claims lesson by listing the 10 wackiest claims or talk about underwriting by showing pictures of houses that would obviously never make it through underwriting. Think of your newsletter like a Reader's Digest issue, lots of fun and helpful information tucked into 3-5 minute articles.

Never try to sell through your newsletter because it just won't work and it will be a huge turnoff to both clients and prospects. People read newsletters for the entertainment and education, not to be sold. The less you try to sell through your newsletter, the more people you'll find contacting you to discuss the information you shared. Concentrate on being the most knowledgeable insurance professional in your client's life and the sales will take care of themselves.

Filling Up Your Newsletter with Good Content

Here we are again, faced with the tough question of what the heck should you talk about and how the heck do you come up with enough stuff to fill a 6 page newsletter every month? Yes, I recommend a 6 page newsletter and no, it won't be tough to fill it up - here's why:

1. Start with your editorial calendar. What one or two topics are on your calendar for the month? What is one of the weekly sub-topics that can be shared in your newsletter?
2. Always include a recipe, it's good for a ½ page of content and people love it (especially if it is something creative)
3. Always include a game, puzzle, riddle or other client interaction section. Make it worth a prize and make it easy for people to play along and you'll get a lot of good interaction.
4. Include a "client of the month" section where you highlight one of your client's businesses and give them some free press. It solidifies your relationship with the business client and gives everyone else a good human interest story.
5. Always include a "thank you" or "welcome" or "referral rewards" section so everyone is reminded that you are bringing on new clients and love referrals.
6. Try doing a book review for a book that somehow relates to the industry or your topic of the month.
7. Use Ezinearticles.com to find pre-written articles and feature it as an article from a guest writer.
8. Use bits and pieces of articles from your other media - your blogs, facebook posts, etc. and then link to the original for the rest of the story.
9. Tell stories about your own life, family, trials, tribulations, successes, vacations, lessons learned, etc. People love to hear about what other people have gone through and what they've learned from the experience.
10. Share "Life Stories" from lifehappens.org or other industry resources.
11. Include an opinion or personal thoughts section about current events so people can get a sense of your thoughts, beliefs and personality.
12. Include stories from the local and national news that may affect your clients or prospects.

I know it seems like a daunting task to come up with 6 pages of content every month, but after you insert the pictures, the header and footer, the big headlines and address section, you really only need about 3-4 pages of content. Every time you come across an article online or get a good question from a client, send yourself an email with "newsletter material" in the subject line and then put it into a special folder where you can keep all of your ideas. Before you know it, you'll have dozens of emails full of content and ideas ready for future editions of your newsletter. When you talk to a client who has a good story to share or a good experience with your office, ask them if you can buy them a cup of coffee and do a quick 10 minute interview so you can share their experience with everyone else in your database.

Just like you do in your blog, find ways to allow clients and prospects to raise their hand and request more information about the topics you cover in your newsletter. Direct them to your blog or have them send you an email for a free report or white paper. Clients will come to you and buy when they are ready to buy, especially if you give them multiple opportunities each month to get more information about specific subjects they are concerned about or interested in.

Some Extra Help for Those That Need It

If you'd like to see a few more examples of my newsletters, visit BestAgentIdeas.com and click the book owners tab. The password is **communication**. If you think you need additional help in building your newsletter or filling it up in a personal way, you'll find some extra resources available on the site as well.

If your blog is the center of your 21st Century Communication universe, your newsletter is the scout that is venturing out into new territory and making contact with new territories. Your newsletter, although not very 21st century, is a vital part of your overall communication plan and because it is a more traditional, old-school method of communicating that most professionals have gone away from, it will really stand out and get noticed by your clients and prospects. Don't neglect your newsletter or give in to the thinking that it is too tough or time-consuming. If you do, you'll be giving up on one of the best ways you have to increase your sales, retention and referrals all at the same time!

AGENCY MAILINGS - WHAT WAS OLD IS NEW AGAIN

When you hear the word "mail", you're probably thinking that there's nothing 21st century about it, but you'd be wrong. 21st Century Communication is all about using tools that are different, unique and set you apart as THE "go to" insurance agency in town. A properly done mailing definitely fits that description and can actually be one of the best producing tools in your toolbox. Here are a couple of reasons why. First, most businesses don't use direct mail anymore. They've gone the way of Google searches and paperless communication so the amount of real mail that people get each day has gone down significantly. Receiving mail from an insurance agency (other than a declaration page or bill) is even less likely. Second, when a business does choose to send a mailing to their client database, it is typically a **boring form letter, a coupon** or **complete junk that goes straight into the trash**.

Those types of mailings are NOT 21st century, they're old-school, played out and ineffective. Those are not the types of mailings we're going to talk about or use with our clients and prospects. The truth is that people still love to get the right kind of mail - especially the type of clients and prospects you're probably working with in your agency. Stop for a second and think about your ideal client. They obviously prefer human interaction to shopping online or through an 800 number or they wouldn't be working with your agency. They are most likely family oriented with a couple of kids, homeowners with two incomes, ages between 35 and 65. They value relationships and their kids' education, they contribute to their 401K and they're responsible with their money. They want professional advice when it comes to protecting their assets and preparing for the future. They're busy with work, hobbies, kids, church, etc. so they want someone watching over their insurance. They live in the better zip codes in town, have quite a few friends, they are involved in something where they can give back and contribute a little (the PTA, little league, Harley Owners Group) and they enjoy getting mail from people they know.

If that sounds like your ideal client (it was a description of mine), keep them in mind for a minute because we're going to come back to them. In case you missed it, the type of person who wants to work with an insurance agent enjoys receiving mail from people they know. A birthday card, thank you note or something personal from a friend on the other side of the country gets them excited about opening their mail. If you do things right, they'll feel the same way about the mail they receive from you. The key is mailing them something they can get excited about. BUT, you say, do agency mailings WORK? More specifically, do they work just as good or better as the other 21st Century Communication tools in our toolbox? The answer is an absolute YES!

According to a study conducted by Millward Brown called *Using Neuroscience to Understand the Role of Direct Mail* (8), physical media leaves a deeper footprint in the brain than digital media. Here are a few of their findings:

- Physical material involves more emotional processing, which is important for memory and brand associations
- Physical materials produce more brain response connected with internal feelings, suggesting greater "internalization" of the ads
- More processing is taking place in the right retrosplenial cortex when physical material is presented. This is involved in the processing of emotionally powerful stimuli and memory, which would suggest that the physical presentation may be generating more emotionally vivid memories

In other words, people connect with direct mail more than with digital communication. At the end of the day, we're all human and humans need to stimulate all 5 senses - direct mail does a better job of doing that for your clients and prospects. Here are some other interesting tidbits about direct mail:

- In a study of the most effective customer acquisition strategies, direct mail finished first (34%), followed by email (25%) and then search engines (10%) (9).
- According to a recent survey conducted by Target Marketing magazine, the media that delivered the strongest ROI for customer acquisition for B2C marketers was direct mail. Direct mail also scored the highest among B2C marketers for customer contact and retention (8).
- Google, the world's largest online marketing company, drives a great deal of business through its direct mail campaign. You've

probably received one or more of their postcards offering a free evaluation of your online marketing (see postcard sample on next page).

No matter how you slice it, a well done piece of mail goes a long way with your clients and prospects IF you are creative with what you send. A corporate form letter or brochure won't do much for you. You need to send things they don't see every day. There are books, courses, seminars and clubs dedicated to the art and science of successful direct mail campaigns. While I won't have the room to cover everything involved in becoming a direct mail guru, it is important to share a few important lessons and action plans to get you started with one of the most important tools in your 21st century toolbox.

How to Run A Successful Agency Mailing Campaign

It is very important to have a plan for your mailing BEFORE you start writing any letters. What are the most important points you want to cover? What do you want your mailing to accomplish? What is the next step you want the reader to take? Where does the mailing fall in your overall plan with your editorial calendar? What happens if people don't respond to your first mailing? A good plan will help you answer all of these questions. The last question, what happens if people don't respond to your mailing, is one of the more important questions you need to answer.

Historically, direct mail only gets a 1% - 3% response rate, but having a good follow up plan can really boost those numbers. While mailing one letter and then never doing any follow up isn't completely worthless, it's pretty close. To increase your response rate, always plan on running your agency mailings in sets of threes - an initial mailing with two follow ups. Some people need to see and hear something numerous times before it catches their attention and becomes worth paying attention to. A second follow up mailing acts as a multiplier on your client's radar. A third follow up is a multiplier of a multiplier and is even more effective at getting your clients and prospects to stand up and take notice of what you're doing.

It's important to not just mail the same thing 3 different times, and you always want to come across as helpful and not pushy, but there are plenty of ways you can reach out to people without coming off as a salesman. We'll go over a few throughout the rest of this chapter. While there are an infinite number intricacies, rules, psychological triggers and formulas in a professionally run mail campaign, there are really only three things you need to worry about to get started with your first agency mailing:

1. Your reader avatar
2. Getting your mailing opened
3. Getting your message read and acted on

You could spend the rest of your career mastering your mailings but the good news is that you don't have to. Fortunately there are so few businesses (especially insurance agencies) that mail anything worthwhile, that it does not take much to impress your clients and prospects. All you have to do is be a little unique and different in order to stand out.

Step One: Your Reader Avatar

Do you remember my ideal client that I shared with you a minute ago? Knowing who they are and everything you can about them is step number one in creating mailings that get great results. Before you ever write a letter or buy any postage stamps, you **must know who you are mailing to.** In fact, the list is every bit as important as the letter. When your client or prospect receives something from you in the mail, they need to feel that the letter was created and sent specifically for them. The more they relate to what they read, the more successful your mailing will be. In order to help make sure they feel the love in your letter, its important create a client avatar.

A client avatar is a representation of your ideal client; the client you are planning on mailing to. My ideal client avatar has a face, a name, a family, a home…an entire life that I try to know as much about as possible. To be clear, it's a fictional face, name, family, home and life but it represents my ideal client. I have a picture I use to represent them that I look at when I am putting together a mailing that they will receive.

My ideal client family avatar

I know that when my mailing arrives, Travis and Mary are going to be hanging out in the front yard talking to their teenage daughter (Susie) about her plans for the weekend and watching their son (Johnny) ride his skateboard. I know who is going to be reading my letter before I ever write my first word and I know what's important to them so I can craft a message that they will relate to, understand, enjoy and most importantly, take action on.

Every time you are going to send an agency mailing, create an avatar for the person or family that will receive it. If you are sending a general letter to your entire client database, try to break it down into groups with similar characteristics and then customize your mailing for their group. A general mailing about mortgage protection will not have the same appeal to everyone you send it to. Grandparents who have 5 years left on their mortgage will think about things completely different than the 30 year old couple who just bought their first home. If you make a few adjustments to your mailing and send one version to the grandparents and another version to the young family that addresses where they are in their life and what's important to them, your mailing will be far more successful.

Step Two: Getting Your Mailing Opened

How many pieces of junk mail do you get on a daily basis that never even gets opened? You sort your mail standing in front of the kitchen trash can and every piece of mail that looks like the same old junk is immediately thrown in the round file, never getting the chance to be opened, read and acted on. This is the worst case scenario for your agency mailings. They come across as junk and immediately get tossed aside. You may be thinking that your clients or prospects would never throw away anything that you send them without at least checking it to make sure it's not important policy information. That MAY be true but if you start sending more and more agency mailings in the same old boring agency envelope, it won't take long before your mail gets set aside. It's like the boy who repeatedly cried wolf. It doesn't take long before people stop paying attention.

In order to guarantee that your clients and prospects read what you send them, you MUST get them to open every piece of mail you send them. In order to get your clients and prospects to open every piece of mail you send them, you MUST get them interested, curious or excited about what they receive before it ever gets opened. You have to be creative in the way you package your letter. You can make your mailing seem official, you can personalize it, you can make it bulky or fun…the options for packaging are limitless. Here are a few ideas to help get your creative juices flowing:

Did you know that an old-school popcorn bag will work like an envelope and even uses the same postage as a regular envelope? If you received a popcorn bag in the mail wouldn't you open it just to see what's inside? Instead of sealing the bag with tab stickers or tape, I created a message using a large mailing label that adds to the popcorn themed package. The front of the bag is pretty much just empty space so there's plenty of room for your mailing label and postage. I didn't include any other messages on the front but there is enough space to add one if you wanted to.

Popcorn bags aren't the only kind of bag that works like a regular envelope and costs the same to mail. You can also use a brown, paper lunch bag, like the kind you used to take to school.

To keep the bag closed I used a large mailing label with a message that was congruent with the packaging that read "there's no such thing as a free lunch." The front of the bag works perfect for the mailing label and postage.

You can get just as creative with regular envelopes as well. There is a lot of white space on an envelope that can be used to add messages or personalization. The post office doesn't have any rules stating you have to leave your white envelope all white.

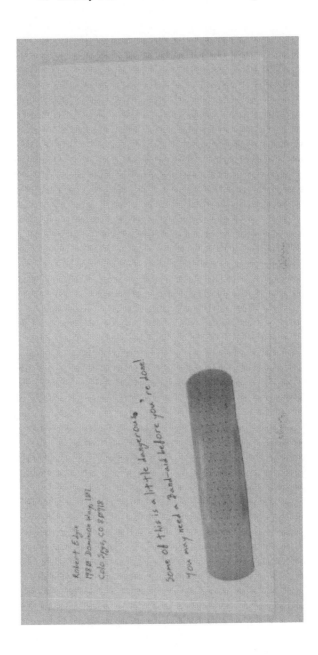

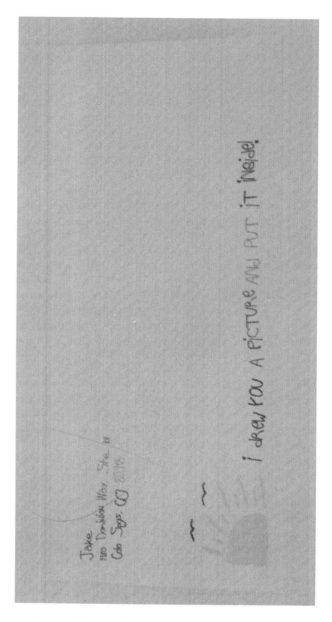

Yes, that's a band aid (actually, it's a very good quality picture of a band aid) on the first envelope and a kid's crayon drawing on the second envelope. There aren't even any rules saying you must mail an envelope with the address and postage on the front. I once filled the address window with shredded money and put all of the mailing information on the back side of the envelope. There was a message right above the window that said "stop throwing away your hard earned money." There were no problems with delivery and no complaints from the post office. If you received an envelope like this one wouldn't you at least want to see what the shredded money was all about?

These are just a few of the things that are possible when you sit down and get a little creative. You can also send birthday card or invitation type envelopes and hand address the envelope so they look personal. You can put something inside of your envelope that makes it lumpy or bulky so people will want to open it and see what's inside or you can mail in a box or UPS envelope for special mailings.

The goal is to do something - anything - that grabs your client's or prospect's attention and makes them excited to open your mailing and see what's inside. That doesn't mean you can't mail a normal agency envelope sometimes, but if that's all you ever mail, you won't get nearly as many opens from the people who receive your mailing and if they don't open it, they certainly don't read it.

Getting Your Message Read and Acted On

Believe it or not, you've already finished the hardest part, getting people to open your mailing. Now, you just have to get them to read it. Your mailings are sales presentations in written form, so when a client is reading one of your mailings, it is important that it sounds like it is coming from you, the same way that your blog and other writing needs to sound like you. Your clients get used to the way you speak and communicate. It's important that your mailings are congruent with your communication style. As people get more and more accustomed to hearing from you and seeing you speak in different places, keeping the same style and tone in your writing will help them be more accepting of what they receive from you.

You need to make sure that the style of your mailing matches up with the style of the package it was received in. If my band aid envelope contains a letter that never mentions the band aid or ties it in to the mailing, my reader is going to be confused about the packaging and feel cheated when reading my letter. Never include an element on the packaging unless you somehow tie it in to the mailing itself. Here are a few examples of what was inside the different envelopes I just showed you. You should be able to tell, without me ever telling you, which letter was in which envelope.

In addition to the letter that went inside the popcorn bag, there was a free offer printed to look like an old fashioned movie ticket. To keep the popcorn theme going with my follow up communication, I made a postcard as well.

The postcard uses the same graphic, font and style so that there is no doubt it goes along with the first mailing.

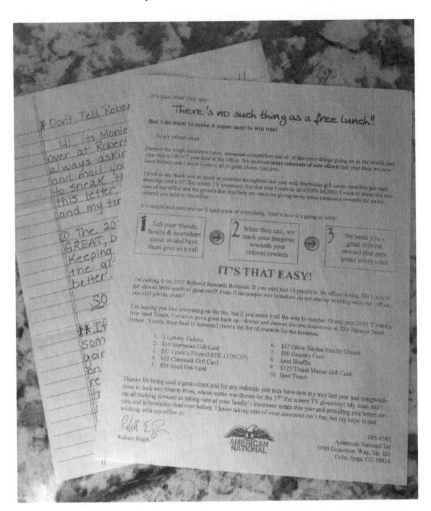

In this mailing, which was obviously sent in the lunch bag, I combined a second letter - a hand written note from one of my staff - to make the mailing more fun, unique and personal. The letter from my staff started with the headline "Don't tell Robert I snuck this in" and went on to offer some pretty great rewards for any referrals that were introduced to our office. Each of the follow up mailings had an additional letter from Monica with an update on what had been going on in the office since the first mailing. For months, I had clients checking in on Monica to make sure she didn't get in trouble for her extra contribution to my letter.

Has the economy gotten SO BAD that Robert got a second job delivering pizzas?

At first glance, it might not look like the follow up postcard to the lunch bag mailing ties into the theme, but the back reveals that there really is a free lunch and I'm delivering it.

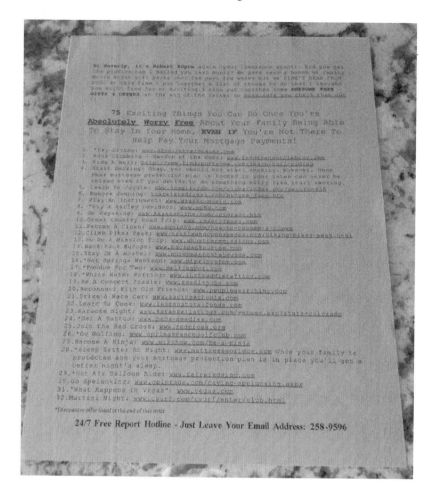

24/7 Free Report Hotline - Just Leave Your Email Address: 258-9596

The band aid envelope had a list of 75 local things you could do (quite a few of which might require some band aids when you were done) once you took care of your family's life insurance. Each of the 75 activities had a link to the website where they could get more information and we even made arrangements with some of the vendors to provide discounts for our clients who wanted to try them out.

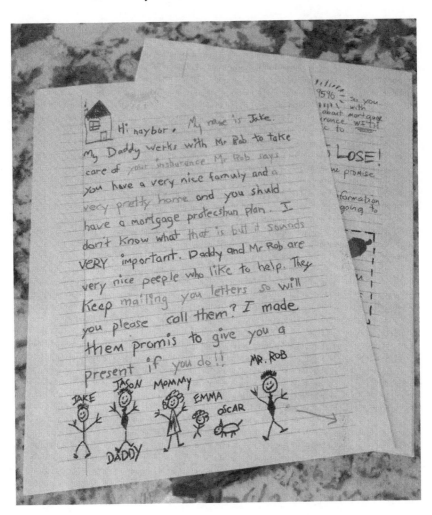

From the cute and creative perspective, the series of letters I sent from Jake (the 4 year old son of one of my staff) is my all-time favorites. Plus, since the letter was hand written by Jake, I added in my own hand written note to go along with it.

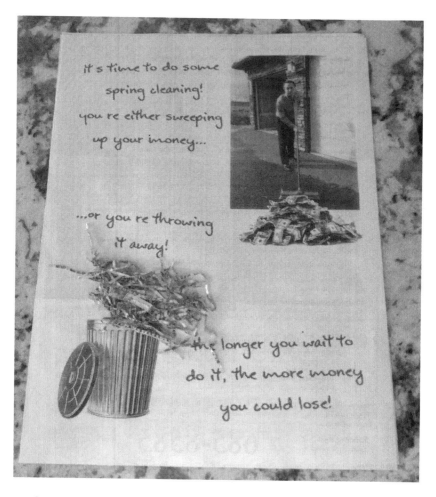

Once unfolded, the money that was showing through the envelope of the window is actually filling up a trash can. The back of the letter keeps the theme going by using the same trash can graphics throughout.

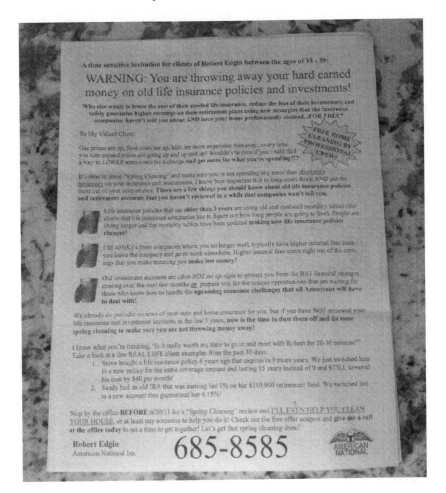

Once you make sure the style of your letter matches or ties into your packaging, you need to craft a message that people will read and act on. We already discussed the importance of really knowing your audience and creating an avatar of the person who will be reading your letter. Knowing what's important to the reader makes it far easier to write about what they want or need to hear about and will pay attention to. Now it's time to learn a few simple copywriting formulas to apply to every mailing you send to make sure you get the best results possible.

When it comes to writing good letters - good copy - there are really only a few simple rules to remember and a few formulas to follow. The first rule is that your letter should have a **Headline**, a **Deadline** and an **Offer**. There's a reason that every newspaper and magazine article have attention grabbing, clearly stated headlines. People need to know what an

179

article (or your letter) is about BEFORE they are willing to invest their time into reading it. You are asking people to make a commitment of their time and energy into reading a page or two and unless you give them a great reason why in your headline, they're not going to do it.

A good **headline** will tell your client or prospect in just a few seconds what reading your letter will do for them; NOT what you are trying to sell, but **what your client or prospect will learn**. The job of the headline is simple: get the reader to read the second line. Be clear about the benefit of reading the letter. What will your client or prospect get out of it? What's in it for them? A good formula to remember for writing headlines is: **End result client wants + specific period of time + address the objections.** An example would be, "Easily attract 2 customers per day without cold calling or rejection." The end result is "attract 2 customers", the specific period of time is "per day" and addressing an objection is "without cold calling or rejection."

Using one piece of the formula (the end result) is okay, using two (end result plus specific time period) is much better and using all three pieces of the formula is GREAT! Here are some more examples of great headlines:

- Hot, fresh pizza delivered to your door in thirty minutes or it's free
- How a new discovery set a family on a path to financial freedom in 30 days
- You can improve your memory in one evening

All of the above headlines tell the customer what to expect in just a matter of seconds. In order to get the best possible headline at the top of each of your mailings, try to be clear and not clever (clarity trumps cleverness every time). Write the headline for one specific person and remember your headline is NOT about your product or service; it's ALL about the person reading it.

To get a downloadable list of the best 100 headlines and a free downloadable copy of the book "How to Write Magnetic Headlines" by the folks over at Copyblogger, go to www.BestAgentIdeas and click the "book owners" tab. The password is **communication**. You'll learn the power of putting together headlines that draw people into your letter, blog or article and see some amazing examples of some of the best headlines of all times.

A **deadline** is next on the list of must haves for an effective mailing. If you want your clients or prospects to do something, you MUST put a deadline on it or it will never get done. I understand you don't want to pressure your clients or make your prospects feel uneasy but if you don't put a deadline on what you're asking them to do, no one will do it. Unfortunately, it's that simple. People are busy living their lives, dealing with problems and taking care of a ton of "to do's" every single day. If you give them one more thing to do but don't put a deadline on it, they will put it off and put it off until they no longer remember what it was they were supposed to do in the first place.

Which do you think will be more effective in getting your client's or prospects to act? **"You're throwing away your hard earned money and spending more than you need to on your life insurance! Call my office when you have some time and I'll mail you a free report on the 6 biggest mistakes that people make when buying life insurance."** OR, **"You're throwing away your hard earned money and spending more than you need to on your life insurance! I have 9 free reports left on the 6 biggest mistakes that people make when buying life insurance. Call today to request your copy before they're gone!"**

A deadline doesn't always have to involve time and it doesn't have to be pushy. A deadline can involve an amount of time, a limited quantity or an extra bonus or incentive. Even if you do base a deadline on responding before a certain date, it doesn't have to be pushy. A deadline gives your clients a reason to move you to the top of the to do list and will always, ALWAYS increase your results. A deadline is even more effective when used in conjunction with the third thing that your letter needs to have, a great offer.

A great **offer** is the catalyst to get your clients and prospects out of their seat and taking action on your mailing. An offer incentivizes people to make an effort and do a little work that they would have otherwise not have had to do. Always remember that you are asking your client or prospect to interrupt their day and do some extra work that they don't have time to do. They're already busy. Talking about insurance or investments is probably not on their list of priorities so any and every incentive you can give them to step out of their comfort zone and make an effort is going to help.

An offer needs to be something of value to your client or prospect but it doesn't necessarily have to cost any money. A free report or white paper, a checklist or educational packet can work if it appeals to the clients wants and needs and would be valuable to them. You can also team up with business clients who are trying to grow their business and offer a limited amount of coupons or discounts to their store. You can offer an experience or entrance to an event, a gift card or any other number of things that will motivate your clients enough to take action. I once mailed a report to all of my clients who were moms on what the financial value of a working mom was as well as the value of a stay at home mom. The report offered them some additional information on the value of a mom and a way to calculate their own financial worth. It also had an offer for a free 60 minute massage so they could take a break and enjoy a mommy time out. I had made arrangements with one of my clients who was trying to grow his chiropractic and massage business to give away a limited number of massages as part of his advertising for new clients. It was a win-win for everyone involved, I got calls from moms who wanted to make an appointment to see me, my client had the chance to talk to potential new clients and the moms got a much needed break with an hour of relaxation and pampering.

Writing Effective Copy

There are literally hundreds of formulas for writing effective copy - putting together a good letter - but you really only need to know two to get started. Before we go through the two formulas that will work wonders with your sales letters, I want to share the four biggest mistakes that most agents make when writing the copy for a mailing. The following was shared by one of my favorite authors, Dan Kennedy, in his book "*No B.S. Direct Marketing*" (a few words have been left out for the sake of space, but the message is the same).

"Most great sales copy is written backwards, from the customer's interests, desires, frustrations, fears, thoughts, feelings and experiences, journeying to a revealing of a solution or fulfillment tied to your business. Most **ineffective** copy starts, instead, with the:

1. Company
2. Product or service
3. It's features and benefits
4. Comparative superiority
5. Price.

These are the five default positions that the overwhelming majority of advertisers, copywriters and salespeople fall back to, rather than developing a more creative, customer-focused positioning. **The first mistake** is to rely on any or all of the five default positions instead of writing to, for and about the psyche of the customer. **The second, closely related mistake**, is writing factually and "professionally" instead of emotionally, with enthusiasm, and conversationally, as you would tell somebody about a discovery you've made. **The third mistake** is being timid or bland in your claims and promises. Many believe that their customers, clients or patients are smarter and more sophisticated than others, at least immune to such sensationalism or hyperbole, possibly offended by it and that they might be discredited if engaging in it. Such business owners would be wrong. Their beliefs are in contradiction with the facts...Zig Ziglar was right, 'Timid salesman have skinny kids.' **The fourth mistake** is letting your copy wimp out at the point of directing the reader, listener, or viewer in exactly what they are supposed to do. If you insist on shouting a weak message louder, you only ruin your vocal chords and dissipate energy. More aggressively advertising a weak message wastes money. You can even do lasting damage by marking yourselves in minds as timid and ordinary and uninteresting...The fact about strong sales copy is that you need it, and you may need to learn to write it for yourself."

Two Copywriting Formulas to Improve Your Sales Letters and Mailings

While I could fill an entire book (lots of people have) on the best formulas for writing good sales letters, you can accomplish just about everything you need to in your agency with just two formulas. It's not that these two formulas are necessarily the most powerful or that much better than any others that are out there but chances are they will be better than anything your clients and prospects have ever been exposed to before. They've probably never been exposed to ANY good sales letter or mailings from their previous insurance agents.

Once you get good at these first two, dive deeper into the subject of direct marketing by reading books like "The Ultimate Sales Letter" by Dan Kennedy and "Advertising Secrets of the Written Word" by Joseph Sugarman. Until then, here are two formulas that will do wonders for your agency:

- **AIDEA** (Attention, Interest, Desire, Evidence, Action)
- **PAS** (Problem, Agitate, Solution)

Attention, interest, desire, evidence, action (AIDEA) has been taught to salespeople since the creation of modern sales and for good reason - it works! The "E" for evidence is one that has been added in over the past few years because people are so cynical about marketing messages that evidence is often needed to get people to act. Here's how AIDEA plays out in successful sales letters:

- **Attention**: You need to be quick and direct to grab people's attention. Use powerful words or a picture that will catch your client's eye and make them stop and read what you have to say next. Too many agents assume that their clients will be interested in what they have to say so they skip the attention step and go straight to interest. This is a big mistake. The best way to get your client's attention is through disruption, a technique that disrupts what your client is doing and jars them into paying attention. It can be done through:

- o Shock factor
- o Personalization
- o Humor

- **Interest**: Once you get your client's attention, you have to get them interested in reading your entire message. This step is actually more challenging than the first. You must stay focused on your client's needs and help them pick out the parts of your letter that are relevant to their lives. Don't bore your client with pages of heavy text. Keep things light and easy to read by breaking up your information with unusual sub-headings, pictures, illustrations and bullet points.

- **Desire**: The interest and desire parts of your letter go hand-in-hand. As you're building the reader's interest, you also need to help them understand how what you're offering can help them in a real way. The main way of doing this is by appealing to their personal needs and wants. You must turn the story you've told into one that is not only extremely relevant to the prospect but also irresistible. Infomercials actually do this very well by showing products in dozens of different situations. "Sure, it's a nice frying pan, but did you know it can also cook a whole roast chicken and do sides at the same time? Wait, it can make dessert too! Plus it's easy to clean and takes up no counter space!" You keep layering on the facts, mixing in come character and persuasiveness until the viewer or reader has only one conclusion - "this thing is definitely for me! In fact, I'm amazed I've been able to live without it for so long!"

- **Evidence**: Most consumers tend to be skeptical about any type of marketing claims. The evidence you use to support the benefit of your letter (whether it is meeting with you, getting a free report, etc.) needs to be compelling and convincing that you're going to provide something of value to your clients. Testimonials about your meetings or report are a great place to start, as are surveys or hard data showing how much good can come to your clients if they follow through with what you are trying to get them to do.

- **Action**: Be very clear about the action you want your client to take and give your client multiple ways to respond. For example, you could allow them to call, email, click on a link, fax a form or visit a web site. This is where your call to action (CTA) goes. Even if your clients have decided that this is not the time for them to act, you at least want to leave a lasting and positive impression on them for the future. That means you need to try and keep your CTA about education, information and advice and not try to force a sale on someone.

The other formula to use with your letters and mailings is problem, agitate, solution (PAS). The wonderful thing about this formula is that it helps you zero in on what's truly important to the client reading your letter. Remember, people make buying decisions (and meeting decisions) based on emotions and avoiding or removing pain usually creates a pretty big emotional response. However, just because someone is aware of their pain doesn't mean there is enough motivation to get them to take action. That's where the PAS formula comes in.

- **Problem**: Everyone deals with a myriad of problems every day, including your clients. Therefore, pointing out a problem (or potential problem) isn't going to be enough motivation to get them off their butt and into your office. However, it is a good place to start. Your client may or may not be aware of their problem but a great sales letter avoids assuming knowledge on the part of their prospect. Set forth the problem in clear, straight forward terms.

- **Agitate**: Once the problem is clearly stated, it's time to whip your clients into a frenzy and make the problem larger than life. One great way to do this is through a story. You can share a story about yourself or another client that shows what happens if the problem goes unaddressed. You can also tell a story of what things might look like in the future if the problem is not taken care of. This still works if the future situation is purely hypothetical; it's the imagined experience that counts.

- **Solution**: Once the pain becomes too much to bear and you can picture your client pacing the room with sweat dripping from their brow, it's time to introduce the solution. Become their life saver. Give them a headache and then provide the aspirin to cure it. Since you want a long-term relationship with your client, this is not the place to push a product or a sale down their throat. This is where you show how skilled and professional you are and offer them the education, information and advice to solve their problem.

Just like every other tool we've discussed throughout the book, it's important to track your letters and find out which ones do the best so you can break down the letter and find out what made it successful. It's also important to remember the rule of three when it comes to your mailings. Before mailing your first letter, have two follow ups ready to go in order to greatly improve your response rate.

It's also important to manage your own expectations. As mentioned, most mailings only have a 1% - 3% response rate. Having two follow ups for a mailing will improve those numbers but there will be times when you send out a letter (or two or three) and get no response. Does that mean that you or your letter has failed? Absolutely not! In fact, letters that do not get a result are still great at reminding your clients of something you do that they WILL be in the market for at some point in the future.

A mailing that does not generate a response can also be a great way for you to learn how to improve your next letter. You weren't an expert driver the first time you sat down behind the steering wheel and you won't be an expert at writing letters right away either. Every letter you write will be better and get a better response than the letter before it. You'll get more creative, have better headlines and come up with some really great offers. Before you know it, you'll be having a blast coming up with your next mailing and your client will be having just as much fun reading it!

SECTION FOUR:

The Next Steps Towards Your Success!

PUTTING IT ALL TOGETHER - YOUR BLUEPRINT FOR SUCCESS

Now that you've learned about **some** of the new tools available to implement in your agency, it's time to step back and look at the big picture. It's time to start putting it all together. Before we do, it's important to know that the tools we've discussed so far are NOT the only tools available to you and it's okay (it's better than okay) if you add in different tools that we haven't discussed.

We've looked at seven great tools to make your communication shine, but tools come and go. They get better, they get replaced, trends change and new technology is invented. Even more important than the specific tools you use to touch your clients is the decision to consistently touch your clients and the commitment to follow through. We've looked at some high-tech tools and some low-tech tools and while the high-tech tools have the "wow factor", the low-tech tools accomplish the same thing - reminding your clients of who you are and what you do.

As important as the tools are to the success of you and your agency, it's ultimately your 21st Century Communication strategy that will make the difference. You have to start thinking more strategically instead of tactically and that's really what 21st Century Communication is all about. You have to start drawing your clients and prospects to you (strategic) instead of constantly having to go chase after them (tactical). Your 21st Century Communication plan is all about making yourself magnetic for your preferred clients and prospects by consistently educating, informing and advising them on the things that matter in their life. In order for that to happen, you have to embrace the most important rule there is for your agency:

Marketing and communicating with your clients are your number one and two jobs in your agency if you want your agency to grow. More important than being excellent at what you do is your ability to market your excellence at what you do.

Some of the best insurance agents and salespeople I've ever known have gone out of business because no one knew they existed. It doesn't matter how much you know about insurance if no one knows who you are or what you do. You have to become the CMO (Chief Marketing Officer) of your agency - TODAY! This, more than anything else in your agency, should be your job and your number one priority. It's okay to delegate tasks to your staff but this is **not** one of the things to delegate. 30% of your work day should be spent working ON your agency instead of IN your agency developing and implementing your marketing and communication plan. I know you're busy doing service work, fixing problems and putting out fires but those aren't the things that will grow your agency. You're working harder instead of smarter.

Working ON your agency instead of IN your agency for 30% of your day is working smarter. You're still working just as hard, maybe harder, but you're working on the right things so that in the future, prospects will come find you instead of you constantly having to go find your prospects. You can't spend all your time working on your business. You still have to put out fires and fix problems. You still have to be tactical and go attack some new business but spending 30% of your time on marketing and communication will help balance out your agency and accelerate your agency's growth. Here's what a typical week looks like for me BEFORE any appointments or meeting are ever set:

My calendar looks the same for the following week except the times are flipped between the morning and the afternoon so that my staff always has the flexibility to schedule client appointments when it works best for the client. Knowing that I will spend 2 hours tomorrow working on retention not only keeps me employed, it keeps me focused on the right things. I'm spending a set amount of time each week working ON my business in order to increase my retention, referrals and grow my agency. Give it a try for a month and see how much you get accomplished!

If you haven't done so already, now is the time to set up your communication calendar for the next 90 days. You should always, always, always have your marketing and communication planned out 60 - 90 days in advance to make sure you have a good, steady supply of information to share with your clients and prospects. I previously gave you a link to download a 3 month sample plan. If you forgot to go look, go to www.BestAgentIdeas.com and click on the "book owners" tab to download it now. The code for the download is **communication**. For your first 90 day plan, try picking two of my sample months and then creating one of your own. Then, for your next 90 days, you'll still have one of mine to use plus two of your own. It's a great way to ease into the process of building your communication calendar.

Having your calendar in place and a communication plan to work will give you amazing confidence heading into the next quarter. I used to wake up every day and hope that I could find stuff to do that would grow my agency. Knowing what to do, when to do and where to do it elevates you to a whole new level. Every other agent in town will be walking into their office tomorrow waiting for things to happen. You'll be walking into yours and making things happen!

Don't feel like you have to jump into using every tool tomorrow. Give yourself time to learn each of the tools and get comfortable using it and then add on another tool. You integrate all of the tools into your agency the same way you eat an elephant - one bite at a time. There are seven tools that you have now learned about and have waiting for you in your 21ˢᵗ Century Communication toolbox. For the first 90 days, I would recommend working on three and leaving the other four alone. You can start with any of the tools that appeal to you but **I would recommend starting with your blog (BL), your Facebook page (FB) and your video mail (VM).** Your blog will get you comfortable with writing and your writing style, your Facebook page will help you get social and your video mail will really get your clients and prospects to sit up and pay attention to what you have to say. It will also help you get comfortable in front of a video camera and seeing yourself on your computer screen talking.

Those three tools work wonderfully well together and act as a great base to your communication plan that all of the other tools can build on. Twitter is an easy extension of Facebook, YouTube is the natural progression from your video mail and your newsletter and agency mailings will be much easier once you've gotten the hang of writing your blog.

Don't overwhelm yourself by trying to do too much too fast. If you get frustrated and quit before things get rolling, you're cheating yourself out of a more successful agency and dooming yourself to a lifetime of hard work with mediocre results. It's much better to never get past one or two tools than to try and implement all seven and end up giving up on all of them. Start off slow and steady. Try to remember that slow and steady ultimately wins the race.

Within the next 7 months, you should have all of the tools in place and within the next year, you'll be seeing some amazing results in your agency. You'll be amazed at how often your clients get a hold of you to buy things and how many times each month there are new referrals who want to see you. Your retention will start to climb within the first three months and should get steadily higher as you continue to implement your 21st Century Communication plan and use more tools. By this time next year, you'll have all of the other agents in your region asking for your secret and wondering why your production and retention are both up - regardless of what your company or the market is doing in your area.

All you have to do is not give up! Make a 12 month commitment right now to being a 21st century agent by using a 21st Century Communication plan and the tools that you've learned about to grow your agency. Open up your calendar and block out the time you need to work on your agency and put your plan into place. You've been given the resources, the tools and the information to succeed. You've been handed the keys to the most successful agency in town – yours. Now, all you have to do is implement them.

Yes, you're going to have to work, but this is going to be the most rewarding work you've done in a long time. I know you've got it in you to get it done. If you didn't, you never would have read this entire book. I can't wait to hear from you throughout the year and share your successes with you. Find a few more agents in your area or in your company that are ready to take their agency to the next level and start developing your communication plan and calendar together. Things are easier when you've got some support along the way. If you stumble or fail with one of your communication pieces, that's okay too. Even a failed communication piece reminds your clients of who you are and what you do.

If you need a little help or encouragement you can email me at Rob@BestAgentIdeas.com and I'll do my best to help. You can also get some more ideas, support and help at www.BestAgentIdeas.com.

The next 12 months are going to be great and you're going to do great. You're on your way to being the most successful agent in town and

I'm excited for all you're about to accomplish. Good luck with the journey and make it a great year!

ADDITIONAL RESOURCES

As a book owner, you can access downloads and bonus material at www.BestAgentIdeas.com and clicking on the "Book Owners" tab. The password for the page is **communication**.

ABOUT THE AUTHOR

Robert Edgin has been in the insurance business since the first grade, when he started helping his father in his Allstate office. He grew up learning the business, spending afternoons and weekends servicing policies and assisting clients. He got his property, casualty, life and health licenses at the age of 19 and opened his own Allstate agency. An entrepreneur at heart, Robert knew that he had to treat his agency like a business. That mindset helped achieve the Rookie of the Year award for Allstate as well as multiple agent of the year awards.

Robert still works in his agency every day; in the trenches to improve and perfect different sales tools, letters and methods of communicating with clients and prospects. He is a consistent top achiever with American National Insurance.

Robert is married to Kylah and has two children, Taylor and Christian. He believes life is meant for living and not just working, and he spends as much time as possible living life to the fullest with his family. An avid scuba diver, hiker and camper, Robert loves the outdoors and looks for adventures that he can share with his family.

At 38 years old, Robert is already a seasoned veteran in the insurance industry. He continues to spend every day trying to grow and improve and share what he learns with everyone he can.

THANK YOU'S

This book is all about learning new things, new tools and new ways to grow and improve. It's dedicated to everyone in my life who has taught (and continues to teach) me new things, new tools and new ways to grow and improve my life.

Thanks, dad, for being a great example of what an agent should do and be for his clients and thanks for helping me branch out on my own at such a young age, supporting me every step of the way. Thanks, mom, for teaching me the value and importance of truly caring for people regardless of what they can do for you.

My wife, I've learned more from you than I can ever thank you for. You continue to help me grow and improve every day and in every way. Thank you for not only helping me be better but for being my reason to want to be better.

Taylor and Christian, your motivation and drive to be the best at what you do is inspiring and a true joy and blessing to watch. Thank you for being great kids and great people and continuing to share your life and adventures with me.

BIBLIOGRAPHY

1. **US Department of Labor.** Bureau of Labor Statistics - Insurance Agents. *BLS.Gov.* [Online] http://www.bls.gov/ooh/sales/insurance-sales-agents.htm.

2. **Thomas, Lynn.** Customer loyalty and retention primer. *RoughNotes.com.* [Online] http://www.roughnotes.com/rnmagazine/search/management/98_0 2P60.HTM.

3. **Hogshead, Sally.** *Fascinate: Your 7 Triggers to Persuasion and Captivation.* New York : HarperCollins, 2010. 978-0-06-171470-2.

4. **McCormack, Mark.** *Quotationsbook.com.* [Online] http://quotationsbook.com/quote/16193/#sthash.ePMeHQQg.dpbs.

5. **AllFacebook.com.** *The unofficial Facebook blog.* [Online] http://allfacebook.com/how-many-pages-does-the-average-facebook-user-like_b115098.

6. **YouTube.** YouTube Statistics. *YouTube.com.* [Online] http://www.youtube.com/yt/press/statistics.html.

7. **Jeffrey, Brian.** Know when to quit but don't quit too soon. *EyesOnSales.* [Online] http://www.eyesonsales.com/content/article/know_when_to_quit_b ut_dont_quit_too_soon_repeat/.

8. **Millward Brown Case Study.** Using Neuroscience to Understand the Role of Direct Mail. *MillwardBrown.com.* [Online] http://www.millwardbrown.com/Libraries/MB_Case_Studies_Downl oads/MillwardBrown_CaseStudy_Neuroscience.sflb.ashx.

9. **Target Marketing.** B2C Marketers Say Direct Mail Delivers Best ROI. *MarketignCharts.com.* [Online]

http://www.marketingcharts.com/wp/print/b2c-marketers-say-direct-mail-delivers-best-roi-21278/.

10. **Forbes.** *Forbes.com.* [Online] http://www.forbes.com/sites/marketshare/2012/03/11/direct-mail-alive-and-kicking/2/.